Advance Praise for *Facing Madame X*

"Jamie Rose has a reverence for this work. She doesn't just know all the Tools; she is someone who has been through hell and used them to come through to the other side. Her willingness to tap into forces inside and outside herself make her unstoppable, and will allow her to help many, many other women be unstoppable as well."

—Phil Stutz, co-author of the *New York Times* bestsellers *The Tools* and *Coming Alive*, subject of the NetFlix docuementary, *Stutz*

"You know that nasty voice in your head, the one that tells you you're not good enough, not worthy, less than? Jamie Rose not only names that voice but also unlocks the secrets to subverting its power. In *Facing Madame X*, Rose shares her own life's journey to illuminate new paths to not just navigate our lives, but reclaim them. Writing with a wise woman's clarity and a truth-teller's fire, the insights she offers are practical, soulful and delivered with the kind of generosity that make you feel genuinely seen. I am recommending this book to every woman I know."

—Samantha Dunn, journalist, author of *Not by Accident*

"Jamie Rose writes with the candor of a memoirist and the precision of a master teacher. This book doesn't just inspire—it arms you with the courage to confront your own Madame X and walk out shining. A rare combination of heart, humor, and hard-won truth."

—Laura Munson, *New York Times* bestselling author and founder of the Haven Writing Retreats

"Jamie Rose is a rare gem. Very few people have her depth of experience with The Tools. Her ability to translate this work—especially through a feminine lens—makes *Facing Madame X* both groundbreaking and essential. This is a book that everyone should read."

—Barry Michels, co-author of the *New York Times* bestsellers *The Tools* and *Coming Alive*

"Jamie Rose's *Facing Madame X* is both an indispensable and practical tool kit for living with intention and a gorgeous memoir of lived-wisdom. Rose writes about her life with verve, pithy insights, and scorching vulnerability. She breaks our hearts while teaching us how to mend our own."

—Annabelle Gurwitch, *New York Times* bestselling author of *The End of My Life is Killing Me*

"In *Facing Madame X*, Jamie Rose gives women a fiercely compassionate roadmap for reclaiming their power from the inner forces that hold them back. With striking honesty and vivid storytelling, she exposes the voice that tells us we are too much, not enough, or too late, and offers tools that are both spiritually resonant and deeply practical. This book shows women how to confront self-doubt, rise with clarity, and trust the life-force within them. It is a powerful and needed companion for anyone ready to step into her fullest expression."

—Claire Bidwell Smith, therapist and author of *Conscious Grieving*

"If you've ever felt alone or 'not enough,' Jamie Rose's beautiful book is a lifeline back to your birthright of universal love. With extraordinary warmth and engaging storytelling, Jamie Rose illuminates a path beyond fear, shame, and loneliness—the grips of Madame X. Rose guides us to act from love rather than fear, reclaim our shadows, and stop neglecting ourselves to meet everyone else's needs. This book feels like a warm embrace you'll want to share with dear friends."

—Dr. Kelli Harding, physician and author of *The Rabbit Effect: Live Longer, Happier, and Healthier with the Groundbreaking Science of Kindness*

"Jamie Rose has written a fascinating, daring, and educational book for women who are ready to heal the shadow sides of themselves. She is a trustworthy guide who walks her talk and teaches from the heart. Highly recommended for women in search of wholeness and healing."

—Judith Orloff, MD, author of *The Empath's Survival Guide*

"Jamie Rose not only takes the idea of 'The Tools' and conceptualizes them for women and the female hero's journey—but delivers a helluva brave, compelling memoir of her own up-and-down life as well. Rose digs way deeper than just guiding us through this save-our-bacon rescue package. She sets it in the context of her own struggles—as actress, wife, therapist, coach, divorced woman—and holds nothing back. Thank you, Jamie, for this fearless, deep dive into what ails all of us . . . and for giving us a tool kit to handle it and thrive."

—Steven Pressfield, bestselling author of *The War of Art*

"*Facing Madame X* is the perfect blend of story, tools, and philosophy. It's a field guide to overcoming, a meditation on the shadows that walk with us, and an acknowledgement of the unique ways we self-sabotage. I left the pages of this book empowered and with a clearer vision of my future and what stands in the way."

—Natashia Deón, author of the critically acclaimed novels *The Perishing* and *Grace*

"I believe feminine energy can change the world—and Jamie has created a brilliant guide that helps women unlock their fullest potential, reclaim their power, and express it in ways that transform their families, their communities, and ultimately, the world."

—Alexandra Jaye Johnson, co-founder of Heroic & Rock Your Goddess Life

"Jamie Rose gives readers real insight and courage, providing a powerful complement to The Tools. These pages contain wisdom for women—and just as much for men."

—Gavin de Becker, bestselling author *The Gift of Fear*

"By weaving raw memoir with sharp psychological insight, Jamie Rose translates the spirit of Phil Stutz's work into the daily reality of women's lives—the pressures, the silencing, the relentless internal (and external) policing. *Facing Madame X* is a powerful guide to reclaiming the inner authority we were never meant to lose."

—Elise Loehnan, *New York Times* bestselling author of *On Our Best Behavior*

FACING MADAME X

Also by Jamie Rose

Shut Up and Dance: The Joy of Letting Go of the Lead, on the Dance Floor and off

FACING MADAME X

THE TOOLS® FOR WOMEN

JAMIE ROSE

Arcade Publishing • New York

Arcade Publishing books may be purchased in bulk at special discounts for sales promotion, corporate gifts, fund-raising, or educational purposes. Special editions can also be created to specifications. For details, contact the Special Sales Department, Arcade Publishing, 307 Fifth Avenue, 4th Floor, New York, NY 10016 or arcade@skyhorsepublishing.com.

Arcade Publishing® is a registered trademark of Skyhorse Publishing, Inc.®, a Delaware corporation.

Visit our website at www.arcadepub.com.

10 9 8 7 6 5 4 3 2 1

Library of Congress Cataloging-in-Publication Data is available on file.

Jacket design by Brian Peterson

Print ISBN: 978-1-64821-043-3
Ebook ISBN: 978-1-64821-044-0

Printed in the United States of America

for my mother

. . . and the shadows

Contents

Foreword by Dr. Phil Stutz xiii

Introduction: Flashback xvii

Chapter One: Meet Madame X 1

Chapter Two: The Joy of Anger 25

Chapter Three: The Mother 43

Chapter Four: Shadow Dancing 65

Chapter Five: The Evil Shadow 79

Chapter Six: Renunciation 105

Chapter Seven: Action 127

Chapter Eight: The Father 153

Chapter Nine: Radical Forgiveness, Loss, and the Sick Shadow 179

Chapter Ten: HIPA and the Divine Feminine 199

Acknowledgments 223

To preserve confidentiality, names and biographical details of clients have been changed.

Foreword
by Dr. Phil Stutz

This is a book whose time has come.

The human race is at a crossroads. Everywhere we look, there's a problem. It's as if our world has broken into pieces and each piece no longer fits. The legal system doesn't provide justice, elections are won by social media, the best medical care is reserved for the rich. The list goes on. Is this the way things are supposed to be?

Or is it the way they always were . . .

Why are these problems so manifest? And why are they so hard to address? *Because they are problems that can only be solved collectively.* The world we live in has been created and sustained by the power of the individual; it isn't equipped to solve problems requiring large numbers of people working together harmoniously.

In our ego-driven society, one's value is proven by having the most power, status, and money. Supported by legacy and social media, the culture echoes and encourages such perverse Darwinism. Billie Holiday sang, "Them that got shall get, them that's not shall lose"—it's natural that those of us who didn't *get* (or get enough) begin to cultivate a sense of cynicism and mistrust in every aspect of life. We've confused competitiveness with success. As they say in Hollywood, "It's not enough to succeed. Your friends must also fail." Too often, we buy into the illusion that there's nothing greater than our own egos; each time your ego can't untie a knot, the illusion weakens. With enough of these failures, one loses all hope. Our high rates of drug abuse, suicidality, and anxiety attest to that.

But things aren't as dire as they seem.

Human beings are capable of meeting almost any challenge, yet only if they act as One. When groups share the same goals, and each individual is willing to sacrifice his personal desires for the group good, an almost mystical force is born. Mythologically, this force is known as the Mother. (Not to be confused with your own.) *This* Mother is an archetype, a paradigm of being in the world. Her connection to human beings is through infinite, unconditional love. The Mother has two special qualities. She heals injuries, physical and emotional, and brings new life, literally and metaphorically, into the world.

Every woman, whether having given birth or not, has a profound connection to that force. Typically, men have been socialized to give the highest value to power, money, *things*—all of which can be measured, competed for, and displayed; however, the energy of the *feminine* is indispensable to our survival.

The world we live in cannot be solved without women taking their rightful, proper place in society. What Jamie Rose talks about in this book is essential. She speaks of women having deep intuitive wisdom and power that they are either out of touch with or afraid to act on. What constrains them? How can they overcome such repressions, whether self-imposed or culturally enforced, in order to seize the power that is their birthright? Women move through the world in pursuit of connection, love, empathy, justice, and wholeness. How can they learn to uncover, nurture, and consciously—actively—accept their destiny?

Jamie has led many women on this journey of embracing the power that belongs to them. I've seen it with my own heart and eyes. Most importantly, she has *lived* this experience herself and used the Tools in an extraordinarily original way. She's dedicated her life to sharing her knowledge, not just by talking about it, but by taking the actions necessary. *Facing Madame X* spells those actions out in such a way that you will have no question about what to do or why you're doing it. Jamie Rose has lit up the tools from a feminine perspective.

And for that, I am deeply grateful.

Introduction
Flashback

In 1986, I was a wild-haired, wild-brained ingénue, starring in her own television series. I had money and a house off Mulholland Drive. I'd just gotten married to a successful screenwriter. I was four years clean and sober—and out of my mind.

As soon as we wed, I wanted to be single. When I got famous from my role on the primetime soap *Falcon Crest*, I immediately thought *film* was where it was at. My recreational activity was fighting with my husband and compulsive shopping. I had a warehouse of power suits and shoulder pads; hey, it was the '80s. At the end of a long, hard, self-obsessed day, I'd hole up in the bedroom with my journal, writing shitty poems that romanticized my fears, showcased my whining, and exalted my anxiety. When I left *Falcon Crest,* I starred in a cop show called *Lady Blue*. Six months later, my agent finally booked me on *The Tonight Show*. When Johnny Carson asked me about *Lady*, I couldn't lie. "It just got canceled."

All that isn't exactly a tragic narrative—I get it—but it sure felt like one at the time.

I didn't have any idea of who I was or what I wanted. I began to choke at auditions. I forgot my lines and started shaking in front of producers and casting directors. My husband filed for divorce. I was a has-been at twenty-seven.

I tried talk therapy. When that didn't work, I did affirmations, chanting, visualization. I saw astrologers and psychics, threw the I Ching and rune stones, had tarot cards and tea leaves read. Nothing helped. Then a friend from acting class raved about a great "no bullshit" psychiatrist she'd had some sessions with—Dr. Phil Stutz. I thought, What have I got to lose? I wouldn't need to *prepare* for my role as patient; by then, I had my shrink monologue down, so it was easy. Seeing a new therapist was like an audition where I'd already gotten the part. It was theater; I could do the play for one night only then close the show, or I could have a longish run. My mind, my choice! I went into his office fully confident that I'd wow him. I was blathering about how I'd been victimized by Hollywood, my horrific childhood, my alcoholism, *blah*, when he interrupted with—

"Okay, *shut the fuck up*."

My jaw dropped.

At the same time I felt the shock of his words, I realized that I wasn't offended—I was *relieved*. On some level, I knew my endless talking about my problems was killing me.

Over the next few years, Stutz saved my life. He taught me a slew of techniques that gave me access to forces that helped create real change in my life so I could throw myself out of the endless *Why me?* loop and get into what he called Forward

Motion. As a young psychiatrist at Rikers Prison and in private practice, he grew frustrated with traditional therapeutic modalities; he felt like he was failing his patients. They'd come to him with the same issues and Stutz would put on the costume of the textbook couch shrink, quietly listening without giving direction. He'd guide them back to their childhood, helping them identify the origin of trauma patterns. Eventually, clients would have a so-called breakthrough and see the "connections." Now that the vicious cycle had been illuminated, they were certain they'd be able to break the cycle. Come next week, they were back at square one. Both Stutz and the people he was trying to help were trapped in the fifty-minute Sisyphean hour. He was at a crossroads.

Stutz desperately wanted to give his patients something to take with them when they left his office—tangible resources that would bring them relief and propel them forward in their lives. In a creative act of desperation (and revelation), Stutz mapped out what he eventually called The Tools®—short meditations that clients could do in only a few moments that allowed them to move from concept to action.

Immediately, he noticed improvement. Patients began to experience real and lasting change, unfettered by neurotic inclinations and setbacks. He noticed as well that despite their best efforts, many reverted to the same old same old, as if a powerful force was intent on paralyzing them—a force that wanted them held back and broken. I've seen the same phenomenon time and again with the clients I work with, and I am convinced that all of us face an unseen but aggressive spiritual opponent intent on sabotaging our growth.

Stutz called that opponent Part X.[1]

Long after he moved to Los Angeles, the actor Jonah Hill saw him in therapy. Jonah's documentary about Stutz was a Netflix hit and brought new attention to his life-changing Tools.[2] Because of his work with those in high levels of the film and television industry, Stutz soon became known as "an open secret in Hollywood." His methods were simple enough to be revolutionary: Stutz offered a dynamic, results-oriented set of practices that built self-trust and integrity, allowing his clients to handle short- and long-term crises.

To be succinct, the Tools *worked.*

I know this firsthand because I've been practicing and teaching Stutz's work for over thirty-five years.

A long time after ending our therapeutic relationship, he suggested that I train as a coach who specialized in the Tools. We now present workshops and seminars together all over the country. Apart from that, we are dear friends. Because of our close ties, he's given me access to material that's never been publicly shared. My contribution is to actively bring a woman's perspective to Stutz's philosophies and practices. While he believes in the power and necessity of the Divine Feminine (and incorporates it in his teachings), *Facing Madame X* is the first time the Tools have been presented in a way that addresses the unique challenges only women face. That the origin of

---

[1] In the '80s and '90s, Stutz used to record all his sessions on cassettes so that clients could listen to the dialogue between appointments. I labeled my collection of tapes. After one particularly unhinged session, I scrawled "Madame X" on the cassette, planting the seeds of what became this book.

[2] His *New York Times* bestseller *The Tools*, cowritten with Barry Michels, continues to sell long after its publication in 2011.

those methods came from a man is irrelevant; Stutz doesn't claim ownership. "They come from the Field," he likes to say. (More about that later.) The Tools are genderless. Having said that, and meaning it, I *will* add that a woman's use and interpretation of them are different then a man's. In *FMX,* I will also be outlining and elaborating, through a woman's perspective, Tools that have never before been published, as well as new ones I've developed in my coaching practice.

These pages contain *Tools for women.*

Tools for living.

Tools for facing Madame X.

Chapter One

Meet Madame X

We never know how high we are
Till we are called to rise;
And then, if we are true to plan,
Our statures touch the skies.
—Emily Dickinson

The greatest trick the devil ever pulled was convincing the world he didn't exist.
—Charles Baudelaire (popularized in *The Usual Suspects*)

Know Your Enemy

Coursing through the veins of every human being is a life-force, a powerful and mysterious energy that keeps our hearts beating and pushes us forward. The Hindus call it prana, the Chinese, qi. In Hebrew it's *ruach*, meaning wind, breath, spirit. What does this force want? More life! Like the universe itself, this energy seeks infinite expansion and the push toward eternity. But there's a counterforce that has one agenda: *to destroy you*.

Stutz calls this "death force" Part X.

X tells the alcoholic the next drink will do no harm; the gambler who's lost their life savings to make one more bet; the job seeker that they're not good enough; the social media addict that the number of "likes" is a barometer of their worth. Just as all human beings possess a life force, our constant companion is the counterforce, Part X. As a cultural consequence, this death force has evolved exponentially (social media is *not* our friend), nurturing laser-focused, pernicious ways in which to attack women.

X praises some of us for *aging gracefully*, while criticizing others for having "too much work." "Antiaging," "slut," "cougar," and "whore" are part of the normalized dialogue around us, often leveled by women themselves. No matter how we look, dress, talk, act, or *think*—it's wrong. It's never enough. It's . . . *unfeminine.* In positions of leadership, women are often criticized for acting like men. Working moms are casually shamed or indicted for not spending enough time with their kids; women who decided not to marry or have children are defective. Too fat, too independent, too old, too mercurial. Too loud, skinny, stupid, or lazy. Too plain . . . too sexy. We're accused of looking hideous for not wearing any makeup and accused of looking hideous for wearing too much. The result? We become Part X's female counterpart and partner-in-crime.

We become Madame X.

MX is cunning. She pretends to be your friend and advocate, warning you not to take risks or rock the boat, cloaking her comments in partial truths and pessimistic logic. You may not be at your ideal weight, but she'll whisper (or shout)—"You're *fat*! A loser! Unlovable!" If a business venture doesn't work out, she'll shout (or whisper) that any future project will fail. Madame X is the voice with the hypnotic mantra of *You can't.* Her goal is to extinguish the radiant light and power every woman carries in her soul.

How can we dampen the whisper so that it's easier to ignore?

How can we still that voice—and crush Madame X?

A client of mine, Melissa, is in her late thirties. Married, with two children, she's a fashion designer and social media influencer with 250,000 Instagram followers. At our first session, she said that she was lazy and needed help increasing her productivity. I told her what she *really* needed was downtime. Her response was, "On Sundays, after breakfast with Dave and the kids, I sometimes don't get to work until noon. Workwise, it's kind of the worst day for me."

Madame X had her by the throat.

Sarah is a Millennial who longs for a romantic relationship. Despite her warmth, superb sense of style, wit, and intelligence, she won't online-date or go on blind dates set up by loving friends because "I'm too fat. All my friends are getting married but I'm *embarrassed* by how I look. Unless I lose twenty pounds, it's *over.*"

Without realizing it, Madame X was Sarah's blind date—and they were a match!

Katherine just turned sixty. With critically acclaimed novels under her belt, she's never had a bestseller. She has a contract for a new book with a respected boutique publisher but is having a bad case of writer's block. Every time she sits down to work, she hears a voice: *No one reads your books, so what's the point?* I shared with Katherine that most of Emily Dickinson's work (one of my favorites) was written *secretly*—only about ten of her poems were published while she was alive. When she died, the poet's sister found over 1,800 poems, some of them bound by Dickinson herself. Everything we know informs us that she didn't *care* about readership. Not all writers are the same—many care deeply—but to become defeated by one's fantasy of readership or popular acceptance is the real tragedy.

What if the world had never learned that "hope is a thing with feathers"? What if Madame X had plucked them all out, whether Emily Dickinson wanted readers or not?

How do we conquer that banshee called Madame X? How do we release ourselves from MX's death grip and reconnect with our fiercely feminine life force and creativity?

First, we must learn to recognize her when she shows her distorted face.

THE TOOL
Labeling[3]

The first step in defeating Madame X is to *see* her—and how she insinuates herself into your life. We do this by a process called "labeling." When you have a thought, ask yourself, *Is there truth to this?* Another thing to ask:

Does this thought hold me back or move me forward?

If the thought holds you back, you can be sure it was sent by Madame X.

Melissa

Thought
I'm lazy and unproductive.

Is it true?
Sunday mornings with my family takes away from my productivity. But the reality is that I'm so nurtured by my time with them; it's a great reset that allows me to

[3] The Tools presented in *Facing Madame X* have different authorship. Attribution is presented by the initials P.S. (Phil Stutz), B.M. (Barry Michels). And J.R. (Jamie Rose). "Labeling" is the only Tool without such assignation, as it draws from CBT (cognitive behavioral therapy), a technique that predates Stutz's work.

feel such gratitude—and actually energizes me for the workweek.

Thought
I'm lazy and unproductive.

Does that thought hold me back or move me forward?
It makes me feel exhausted. Like I can never do enough. It makes me feel like giving up.

. . . that thought was sent by Madame X.

Sarah

Thought
As long as I'm overweight, I will never have a relationship.

Is it true?
I'm twenty pounds heavier than I want to be. But the only one it seems to bother is *me*—I get loads of compliments on my personal style. Friends whose bodies look like mine are in loving relationships.

Thought
I'm too fat.

Does that thought hold me back or move me forward?
When I hear that voice, I feel ugly and alone, helpless and hopeless.

. . . Madame X speaks.

Katherine

Thought
Why should I write another book when no one reads them?

Is it true?
My books never made much money (like every writer I've ever known). Still, I've had great reviews. I'm so joyful for the readers I have—I get beautiful letters from strangers telling me that my books had a profound effect on their lives.

Thought
There's no point in writing because my books don't sell.

Does that thought hold me back or move me forward?
It stops me from doing the thing I love that makes me feel the most alive. It kills my spirit.

. . . MX strikes again.

Whirl up, sea—cover us with your pools of fir.
—H. D. "Oread"

You must change your life.
—Rainer Maria Rilke, "Archaic Torso of Apollo"

Madame X in Me

At fifty-four, I was in a long-term relationship that looked perfect from the outside. Kip was handsome, kind, funny. We lived in a house on a mountain, with a pool and a tennis court. (It burned down in the Palisades fire long after we separated.) In the beginning, we were great but as the years passed, not so much. I *loved* doing tango. I even wrote a book about the joy that dance brought me because it was such a connected experience—something that was lacking in my marriage. I never cheated, which doesn't make me a saint; I went dancing instead. (As it turned out, it only takes one to tango!) Tango is a late-night event. My husband hit the sack around the time I was heading out in my fringe and stilettos. It didn't bother him. Maybe it should have. I guess it was my Sagittarian nature—I longed for independence and adventure and wound up leading a not-so-secret secret life. I traveled alone to weekend dance conventions and took trips to New York to visit friends and see plays. I'd ask him to come but it was always March Madness or the World Series or football season. Couples have different interests and support one another in their pursuits; that's healthy. But we were competing in the Olympic marital sport of extreme distancing, both intimate and geographic. We weren't having sex. We were fighting all the time.

Kip's parents were raised in the Great Depression and instilled in him their fear of going broke. I learned valuable things from him in that regard because I was a terrible money manager. When we began living together, I was thirty-nine and my acting career had stalled. I made a ton of money in my twenties and thirties but lost it all in bad real estate investments and overspending. Marriage to Kip was a course correction. The course was corrected so radically, I got whiplash. We didn't have a joint house account for monthly expenses. If I wanted to travel or buy a pair of new shoes or even sheets and towels, I was on my own. It was like I was squatting in an Airbnb. Winding through those serpentine hillside streets started to become a weird drive of shame every time I went home.

I had thought of leaving but all I had was a small income from teaching acting and the occasional TV gig. I was afraid that I wouldn't be able to support myself. I confided in an old friend and got a cold shower warning: "When you're fifty-four, the dating game is a massacre. Don't blow up whatever cushiness you have. You'll end up alone."

Cushiness? Yeah, *cushiness.* That's the word she used.

I was shell-shocked.

After that call, I found another cold shower—one of those cushy automated carwashes. As more water got dumped on me, I replayed the scolding in my head. I reminded myself that my husband was great! I mean, he wasn't a cheater, right? He was and *is* a sweetheart. What was my problem? I had a roof over my head and food in the fridge. Was I being selfish to want more? And what was "more," anyway? What did *more* look like? Sharing expenses? Sexual intimacy? As the car was slowly dragged through the crazy buffers, spray-jets, and drying fans, I tried to assess whether any of my fantasies or expectations were selfish or delusional.

What was a happy marriage, anyway?

Maybe what I wanted didn't exist.

Despite my friend's advice, I visited a divorce attorney to see what my options were. After I told her my yearly income, she leaned forward like an older sister and said that I qualified for community property—but since my husband made most of his money before we married and didn't put my name on the deed, "You're not in great shape. I want you to ask yourself, *How bad is the marriage?*" I left that office feeling gut-punched. The lawyer added fuel to my confused, fearful thoughts. She was advocating for me in the best way she could but instead ended up echoing the words of Madame X that I'd been hearing in my head.

I got double-teamed!

I visited a beloved cousin for solace. Michael and I grew up together and he'd known me through all the high and low dramas. After the familiar litany of how unhappy I was—the terror of being alone for the rest of my life and ending up in a tent on the sidewalk—he said, "Jamie! All through your forties and fifties, you've been talking about how unhappy you are in this marriage. Soon, you'll be sixty, then you'll be *seventy*, and you'll be saying the same fucking thing. The truth is that you'll be happier living *alone* in an apartment in the Valley than you are in this Malibu mountain marriage mess." He took a breath. "Don't waste any more of your life."

Jamie

Thought
I'm too old to find another relationship. And if I leave, I won't be able to support myself.

Is it true?
It might be difficult meeting someone at my age, but I feel so alone in this marriage that I may as well be single. I'm still working—or *able* to work. I know I can find a cheap place to live and be able to afford the basics.

Thought
I'm too old to find another relationship. And if I leave, I won't be able to support myself.

Does that thought move me forward or hold me back?
The thought is driven by fear.

. . . *Madame* X marks the spot.

> Everyone knows the expression "reliving a tragedy." What many people are engaged in is pre-living a tragedy.
> —Gavin de Becker

> I have come to believe that all of life is about what we fear. The question is not what will happen when we are afraid, but how will we deal with it. Will we cower or rise up?
> —Audre Lorde

Her Favorite Weapons

Another of Madame X's favorite weapons is negative predictions about the future. She's a soothsayer of fear, a doomsday Cassandra who specializes in worst-case scenarios designed to quash our dreams. Remember, MX has one goal—to stop us from moving forward—to propel us *backward*. She crowds our minds with visions of horrors yet to come. Haunted by the looming specter of a disastrous future, our nervous systems react as if the calamity is happening *right now*. We become paralyzed or make impulsive, fear-driven decisions over problems that haven't occurred. And probably never will.

The only predictable thing about the future is uncertainty. While many of us are black belts in catastrophizing, it's impossible to know whether the ultimate result of a seemingly bad event is positive or negative.

Here's a famous Zen story that illustrates that point.

When an old farmer's horse ran away, his neighbors cried, "What bad luck!" The farmer simply replied, "Bad luck? Good luck? Who knows." A week later, the unruly animal returned—trailed by a herd of wild horses. "What good luck!" the neighbors cried. Again, the farmer said, "Good luck? Bad luck? Who knows." When his son broke his leg trying to tame one of the wild horses, the neighbors shook their heads and said, "Such bad luck!" The farmer said the same thing he always did. Days later, all of the young village men were drafted, dying in battle—except for the farmer's son, who was passed over because of his injury. The mournful villagers whispered, "*What good luck.*"

This time, the old farmer said nothing.

Most of our negative predictions never happen. Still, Madame X convinces us there is value in imagining terrible what-ifs. That worrying will somehow protect us, that rumination is a kind of prophylactic against pain, and if we expect the worst, it won't hurt as much. This is a lie. The obsession with dark narratives creates a chemical stew—a quicksand from which it's difficult to free oneself. In many ways, "future tripping" mirrors the cycle of addiction. Human beings can become addicted to practically anything, including psychic pain. Even if one of MX's prophesies comes to pass, we've already lived through it in our heads—and have to go experience the unpleasant repercussions twice, reliving what has been pre-lived.

Good and bad things happen—that's the nature of life. The useless cycle of drama and trauma serve no one but Madame X. So how do we fight back against her ominous forecasts?

With *reality*.

Lily Tomlin once said that reality was overrated. But in truth, it's one of the most powerful weapons we have to defeat Madame X—so, let's learn a tool that shows us how.

THE TOOL
The Science of Reality
(P.S.)

Get yourself some plain index cards and box to keep them in.

When Madame X makes a dire prophesy, write it down. Write the date and her prediction, then a horizontal line below it. Under that line, write the words *What Actually Occurred*. Then put it away in the box. After a day, a week, or a month, retrieve the card like you're a scientist coming back to look at a slide, noting the changes in an experiment.

Now, write down what *actually* happened.

Below is an example of an index card from my own life.

JAMIE
Madame X Prediction—11/26/2015

I will leave my husband and be miserable, broke, and alone for the rest of my life.

What Actually Occurred—2/16/2016

I'm single and living in a beautiful apartment right next door to my parents. My practice is flourishing and I'm dating a wonderful guy.

~

After talking to my cousin Michael, I faced the reality that I was staying in my marriage for selfish reasons. I was afraid that I couldn't make enough money on my own and that I was too old to attract another partner. There was no exit; the window of another serious relationship had been glued shut and graffitied over.

Along with those thoughts, came others: *My husband deserves better. He deserves devotion and appreciation—a woman who can love him for who he is.* Not only was I holding myself back but I was involved in a betrayal of someone I dearly loved. That night I pulled out an index card, wrote down my fears, and put it in a box. (See page 14.)

When I married Kip in a small ceremony, I cried the whole time—joy! gratitude! relief!—he was the love of my life. *I* had been the one who pushed for marriage. We'd both been married once before and Kip liked to say he didn't want to be "twice divorced." After five years of living together—I was already forty-four and he was fifty-seven—I wanted security. It's strange how many interpretations the s-word can evoke. I didn't want to feel like a guest in his house anymore; I longed for a home, and everything I imagined that word to be. A home that was his *and* mine.

Before my first marriage, I bought a house, then sold it when I got married and used that money to buy a place with my new husband. When we divorced, *that* house was sold and I put my share toward a condo that ended up getting yellow-listed in the 1994 earthquake. I escaped to a rented studio apartment. There's a lot to say about a room of one's own, including that it's a shitty place to entertain friends and family.

And did I mention that right after that, I filed for bankruptcy? Good times!

A couple of years later, I met Kip. He was funny and warm and reminded me of Dad in so many ways. They were both singers; even their speaking voices sounded alike. I thought, "I could build a life with this man." Kip and my father Stewart got along like thespians on fire. Showbiz blood was in their veins and I *loved* that. It so touched me—that homey feeling of an instant family. Thinking about our marriage, my dad still looms.

Was I chasing the home—chasing the father—that I so longed for? The family home, both real and symbolic, that remained elusive, yellow-listed, always achingly out of reach? "Yellow-listed" is an evocative metaphor. In disaster zones, a yellow sticker means that a structure has sustained moderate damage and that it may be used if it poses no hazard; other parts may be entered only under supervision to remove valuables and other property. That's how I feel when thinking about large swathes of my life!

After we'd been dating a while, I began talking to Kip about the future. I was close to forty and wanted to have a child. Kip's daughter was already in college; he wasn't wild about having another kid. He never came out and told me that. Instead, he'd say, "I don't want to be the person who would stop you from having a child." I needed more than that. I didn't want to feel like he was being charitable, and *definitely* didn't want to do it alone. I wanted a husband who was all in. His response left me livid and I ended up walking out. Dad was on my side for a simple reason: he wanted to be a grandpa. But Mom, always the stoic, practical one, had a different opinion. As far as she knew, I'd be exchanging a warm, stable, wonderful man for a life of financial and personal insecurity. She had a samurai way of making me feel childish, which I probably was—add prideful, headstrong, frustrated, and mad as hell about the career cards I'd been dealt.

I still got the occasional television gig but my life as an actress was in the shadows of where it used to be. I began my professional career when I was six years old, and the money I made helped my parents buy our first house. When I was doing well on *Falcon Crest,* I helped them out if they were struggling—but now the tables had turned. They started giving me $500 a month, taking the edge off the rent on the aforementioned room of my own. By that time, they were both working in home improvement sales and living off their commissions. I felt worse than awful; the tables turned so hard that shame knocked the breath out of me.

Over the years, it's remarkable how many female clients have revealed their deepest fear: they'll become invisible, forgotten, and worse—homeless. I've learned that it's a common theme among women and looking back, I started to hear its siren call. Even though I knew in my heart that it would probably mean I would never have a child, I went back to Kip. There are women who find themselves in the situation I was in but go sailing against the traditional wind to become single moms. I wasn't one of them.

After our unbreak-up, we moved in together. The house Kip owned felt too small. Besides, we wanted to pick a place together. We found one in the isolated hills above Malibu. I've already spoken about him never putting me on the deed. I never insisted on co-ownership of the house because I felt that I didn't deserve it. I wasn't a good homemaker. I never really learned to cook . . . I just wasn't interested. My general thought became: *I guess I'm not marriage material.* My husband, also an actor, wasn't working much either but got income renting out his old house. He wasn't rich but had a little nest egg. *A nest egg of his own . . .*

I decided that if I didn't own the place, I could sure do an act-as-if. I threw a lot of shindigs there—potlucks, pool parties, game nights, big family get-togethers. We'd have all the cousins on my Jewish side (over fifty of them!), then all the cousins on my Mormon side (over fifty of them!). We had a huge eightieth birthday party for Dad, who by then had his Alzheimer's diagnosis but still loved to sing. Kip played piano while Stewart belted out show tunes.

To make sense of those times, I think again of my father.

My first love. He was handsome and charismatic and I had a closeness with him that I never felt with Mom. My brother Stephen was a math genius. Dad was super proud of him but only spoke showbiz, and that was a language I was fluent in. I loved helping him run lines before his auditions. Watching rehearsals of theater he did in LA was my after-school activity. But then he would disappear doing summer stock or his nightclub act in Vegas (and even as far as Australia). For a time, as a joke, Stevie and I began calling him "Uncle Daddy" because he felt more like a wildly fun, eccentric visitor than a father. He brought us gifts from wherever he was performing, then *poof*—gone again.

It took its toll on Mom.

When her drinking worsened, I became his main emotional support in a way that Reta wasn't capable of. One time, when the family was in Vegas, my baby brother (eleven then) was asleep in the hotel room while Mom was in the casino, drinking and gambling. Dad wanted to see a show and took me with him. In the crowded hotel elevator, I remember making sure to keep calling him "Dad"—so everyone would know I was his daughter, not his girlfriend. I was thirteen.

Over the years, my relationship with Kip became platonic, like with Dad. I felt safe with my husband in a way I'd longed for since I was a girl. How could I ever leave him? It wasn't just the house I would be abandoning; it was family. The morning Kip's daughter gave birth to her first child, I was part of a group of soon-to-be grandparents in the waiting room. But I felt like an outsider. I wasn't related by blood, and our marriage was in-name-only. I still felt like a houseguest in my own home—*his* home. My visa could be revoked at any time.

I finally got the courage to tell him I wanted a divorce.

I started apartment-hunting and was terror-stricken. I was stunned at how much rents had gone up during my marriage. Even a modest apartment in the Valley was way out of my range. I didn't have a great feeling about what might happen in a divorce settlement. That attorney I saw had warned that I might walk away with nothing.

My parents were retired and Dad's dementia was getting worse. They lived in a modest, rent-controlled apartment building in an *It's A Wonderful Life*–style neighborhood called Toluca Lake. I asked them to let me know if an apartment became available. Mom told me there were never vacancies because, like them, most of the tenants had been there for years. And even if an apartment *did* come up, the landlord would raise the price. I thought about the houses that I'd had and the ones I had given up. I was embarrassed about not having a home—that I couldn't say "Come live with me!" to my parents felt like a failure. Why had I sold the big house on Woodrow Wilson that I bought with my TV money? *What a fool I was, what a terrible child, what a loser—*

Madame X was hard at work.

I became more discouraged and depressed with each day. I knew I was going to be downsizing, but I was looking at places more squalid and run-down than the one I rented when I was eighteen. At my low point, Mom called to tell me that the unit next door had just became available and the owner said she would give it to me at the old, rent-controlled price. It was a huge one-bedroom apartment with two patios and a working fireplace. I had a surge of emotion. Beyond the relief of the housing nightmare ending, I'd just been presented with an amazing gift: the chance to rekindle a broken relationship with the woman who had done her best, under difficult circumstances, to raise her kids. Dad losing his mind and memory made it even more poignant. He was disappearing, like he always did, but almost in a poetic way. Like the assistant in a magic show, I could watch him appear and disappear, until he finally left the stage.

And when that happened, Mom would be standing beside me.

The last time I lived with my parents was at seventeen. I couldn't wait to get out of there. My bedroom was a refuge from the chaos of Mom's drinking. Joni Mitchell and Cat Stevens were on the record player; Emerson, Lake & Palmer posters plastered the walls. Incense masked the smell of pot and cigarettes. That room was all about hanging with girlfriends, sneaking in long-haired crushes through the window, and the bubbling sound of my bong as we passed it around. I spent hours alone there journaling and writing dumb, derivative poems. (Emily D. turned over in her grave.) Mom was getting wasted every night—I think she was more stoned than I was. She was a monster when she drank and I was always the one on the receiving end of her tirades and physical outbursts.

My father was my only source of love and acceptance in the house until one night she even ruined *that*. I was sixteen—yet another night with Drunk Mom. She was on the couch. Dad and I were kidding her about putting down the vodka glass (begging didn't work). Her face filled with rage. She snarled, "If you love your daughter so fucking much, you know what you should do? *You should marry her.*" I froze. I knew that wasn't *her* talking; it was the alcohol. Dad knew that too. Yet, in that moment, she turned our mutual love into something unnatural and perverse.

From that moment, there was no place in our family I was safe.

Now, thirty-seven years later, there I was, back in my room. This time, there were adultish things on the walls. (I still played Joni music.) I was sober, so the only bubbling sound was a humidifier. Mom was sober, too, and had been for decades. The father and husband who had wanted to check out from the obligations and responsibilities of family was at last getting his wish. My brother and sister-in-law lived across town, and because I was down the hall from Mom and Dad, it was natural for me to become the designated caregiver.

The weekly schedule went something like this:

> Costco: √
> Carwash: √
> Providence Saint Joseph Medical Center Emergency: √
> Trader Joes: √

Rinse and repeat.

My father died a year after I moved into the building in Toluca Lake. In 2024, Mom entered home hospice. Something is seared into my memory: I helped Reta up from the flying carpet of her bedroom hospital bed and walked her into the living room, where we joined my brother and sister-in-law Meli on the couch. She had something to say and the room grew quiet.

With an elegant, radiant nobility that made her look twenty again, she pronounced, "I want to be with my husband. And *soon*."

~

For a long time, I believed my mother *was* Madame X.

Then I believed *I* was Madame X.

It became a crazy hall of mirrors: everywhere I looked, I saw the Madame—a grandiose distortion of the truth. We're complicated creatures. We are challenged by the toxic effects of MX but can learn ways to resist, to push back. In that process, Madame X becomes the ultimate Tool; it depends how we *use* that tool.

What does it mean to face her?

I've talked a little about that in this chapter. Let's go deeper.

Chapter Two

The Joy of Anger

No coward soul is mine,
No trembler in the world's storm-troubled sphere.
—Emily Brontë

One must still have chaos in oneself to give birth to a dancing star.
—Friedrich Nietzsche

"Smile!" he shouted as I passed him on the street.

Not only did I not obey his command, but I wanted to throttle him. I fantasized about grabbing the guy by the collar and whispering, "I will—*after you die.*" Instead, I ignored him, and walked on by, as the Bacharach song goes. But anger seethed within.

We are born in a storm of rage. Expelled from the warmth and safety of the womb, we choke our first breaths between furious sobs that cry out I AM HERE! I EXIST!

I'm *alive.*

Men are encouraged to express their anger—or should I say *allowed*—because it's part of their masculine "right," even an indicator of leadership and strength. But women are taught to suppress their rage. We're told that anger is ugly and unfeminine. We've been socialized to be polite, reserved, and "ladylike"—to cross our legs and quiet our voices. When we express rage, we're indicted as hormonal, psycho bitches.

Nasty women.

So we push our anger down. But it doesn't go away. Instead, it becomes distorted. In its corrupted form, anger is destructive. It can express itself in violence, resentfulness, judgmentalism, isolation, or self-harm. It dismantles relationships. The perversion and suppression of anger can lead to a host of physical issues such as headaches, digestive problems, anxiety and depression, even strokes and heart attacks.

In the film *Carrie*, a shy high school girl is controlled by her fanatically religious mother and bullied by fellow high school students. In the movie's climatic scene, her classmates trick Carrie into believing she's been voted homecoming queen. After being crowned, she stands onstage, overcome with happiness—when suddenly a pail of pig blood is dumped on her head in front of the shocked, ecstatic student body. In that moment of nuclear humiliation, her face dripping with blood, Carrie (who has unexplored telekinetic powers) shifts from debilitating shame to all-consuming rage. She takes violent revenge on her tormentors, resulting in their deaths, and eventually her own. Within her is a primal, mythic rage, a vital, animalistic force. If she had been organically connected to that anger, it might have become a driving force behind personal expression and ultimate independence. But it was suppressed. Instead of being a vital asset, it became ugly, pernicious, and suicidal.

One could say that vengeful Carrie is a metaphor for the collective fury generated by thousands of years of the oppression of women's power. In America, as recently as 1974—the year the Equal Credit Opportunity Act was passed—women weren't allowed to get credit cards or loans without male cosigners. As we know all too well, such injustices are still going strong. Today, in Taliban-controlled Afghanistan, and in Iran, under an increasingly authoritarian regime, women can be imprisoned or even murdered by showing their faces or speaking in public. Worldwide, women are trained, by forces brutal or subtle, to disconnect from their power and their rage.

Yet, anger is an essential aspect of human expression. In its pure, undistorted form, the emotion is part of one's birthright, a vital expression of one's unique, cosmic personhood. Used with *intention,* rage is an inextinguishable force that can be a catalyst for personal creativity and growth. But first, one needs to learn how to rage against the machine—the machine of a patriarchal culture that tries, at any and all cost, to erase us.

THE TOOL
Cosmic Rage
(P.S.)

Close your eyes. Picture yourself inside a circle. This is the I AM *space. In it, you feel strong, and powerful. You stand firmly in your unique selfhood.*

Outside your I AM *circle, surrounding you 360°, is another circle. In this circle, imagine Madame X shouting out whatever specific weapons she uses against you—you're stupid, lazy, too old, too opinionated, untalented, fat, unproductive, et fucking cetera. You can also imagine specific people who put you down in the past (family members, exes, frenemies), each attacking you in Madame X's voice.*

Generate a feeling of rage inside your body—make it as intense as you can. Then, like the defensive quills of a porcupine, shoot the rage out from your body in every direction. At the same time, shout (in your mind, or out loud), "Fuck you! I *AM*!" *or* "Get away from me! I *AM*!"

The force of your rage pushes Madame X away and gives you space to fully express your individual voice. You feel powerful and free.

Important note: never *direct Cosmic Rage at an actual person*—always *direct it at the MX force coming through them. Do this by imagining a kind of toxic aura surrounding that person. Direct the rage force at that aura.*

The emotion invoked by Cosmic Rage isn't anger on a human scale. It isn't a variation of what we feel when we're cut off in traffic or stub a toe—it's anger on a *cosmic* level. It's the rage of the Old Testament God who commanded, "Let There Be Light." It's the rage of the Hindu goddess Durga, who uses her awesome wrath to combat evil and empower life. *This* rage is positive, creationary, and expanding. I AM is a soul statement and demand, one that declares our individuality and sovereign right to exist in all our ferocious glory.

~

My client was afraid of her boss.

He wasn't unkind but had a harsh style that Rebecca was intimidated by. She respected him and wanted his approval; as a result, she was hypersensitive to his moods. Any time she interacted with him, even through email, she felt as if she were walking on eggshells.

Rebecca grew up with a demanding and critical father. When she got good grades, he criticized the way she dressed. He thrilled in putting down her choice of friends. No matter how hard she tried, Rebecca always fell short in the eyes of that powerful man. He died when she was thirty-five. Ten years later, she was still replaying her childhood dynamic.

The past controlled Rebecca's present. Her sense of self was completely dependent on the outside world. The reactions and opinions of others jostled her self-worth like the metal balls in the pinball machine that her father lovingly restored and played incessantly in the garage.

Intuitively, I knew that Rebecca's relationship with her boss was a gift. I needed her to understand—to *believe*—that he was providing her with an opportunity to be initiated into the world of adults. It was essential that she used her fear as a portal to maturity. If she could learn to anchor her selfhood in his presence, she would gain a superpower. She could break free of those childhood insecurities and step into the full, dynamic potency of adulthood.

I encouraged Rebecca to do the Cosmic Rage tool as a preventive. Before any interaction with her boss (in-person meetings, phone calls, emails, or even if she was simply *thinking* about him), she was to work the Tool. I told her to close her eyes and place herself in the I AM circle, then imagine herself surrounded by a ring of duplicate bosses. I told her to visualize the clones, all broadcasting her worst fears. *You're not working hard enough! Why can't you solve this problem? You're going to be fired!* Rebecca blasted out her cosmic-level rage to the Circle. Remember, the rage isn't directed at her actual boss, it's directed at the X-force working through him.

The Tool made her feel like she was in an impenetrable fortress, protected from the psychic bombardments of her enemy—Madame X. Within this I AM space, she could detach from the negative story of her past and live in the reality of the present. She soon realized that what she had previously experienced as personal criticism wasn't that at all; it was simply the boss's blunt, no-nonsense style. He was good at his job and expected his team to be the same. Rebecca *understood* that he wouldn't have hired her in the first place if he had doubted what she had to offer. Once she stopped wasting time replaying hurt feelings and imagined shortcomings, her confidence and creativity soared. She reclaimed that original energy and became boldly innovative. Not only did her relationship with her boss improve, but he became her fiercest ally. Who was the boss now? (A year later, *she* was. Literally.)

The Tool couldn't change the trauma of her past but it freed her from its hold on the present.

Book Nerd

I started reading when I was four years old. Books were my refuge. Whatever chaos was happening around me, I felt safe in the world of Story. A book was more than cardboard and paper. It was a luminous, exalted thing. A portal to magic.

As an adult, I loved taking writing classes. I published a few articles and essays but always considered myself a hobbyist. For me, *real* writers existed on a higher plane—*real* writers were wizards who could alchemize words into something far more fascinating, intricate, and alive than reality. In my early forties, right around the time my acting career stalled out, I got an idea for a book. I shared my idea with my friend, the memoirist Samantha Dunn. She loved it and encouraged me to pursue a publishing deal. I told Sam she was crazy. I was an actor, not a writer. Not a *real* writer, anyway—I was a dilletante, a dabbler, a wannabe. Maybe I could write a short article . . . but a book? *No effing way.* But Sam kept pushing. Since my only other choice was to wait by the phone like a mummified ingenue for my agent's call (which rarely came), I decided to follow her advice.

I bought a book with a *For Dummies*–type title—*How to Write a Non-Fiction Book Proposal*—and followed its prompts. Despite a lack of confidence in my writing abilities (understatement!), I dragged myself to my office—a local coffeeshop—and white-knuckled my proposal. Hey, J. K. Rowling wrote her first book in a tea shop overlooking Edinburgh Castle; I wrote in a Starbucks overlooking Universal Studios. Take *that,* Lord Voldemort.

But instead of the Dark Lord, Madame X sat on my shoulder whispering sour nothings of negativity into my ear: "Who do you think you're kidding? . . . You're not a *real* writer . . . You're not even an actress anymore!" I used Cosmic Rage incessantly. I'd scream "Fuck you!" in my mind—and once, accidently, out loud. The mochaccino woman at the next table smiled as she was leaving. With warm, luxurious pity, she asked, "Are you okay?"

And I *was*, because the Tool worked.

After that, everything flowed. Two months later, I got a book deal. I'm not sharing this to say that magic always happens. What I *do* want to share is a nasty axiom: Madame X is a dream-killer. She *lives* to put obstacles up between you and your heart's most precious desire. The greater her attacks, the more she belittles, the more devious she is in thwarting your progress . . . well, those are indicators that you're on your way to something good.

When I sold that book, most of my friends were delighted—but not everyone.

It got back to me that a frenemy had gossiped to everyone in our circle that I must have hired a ghostwriter—for my proposal, no less!—because "We all know Jamie Rose can't write." That hit especially hard because she knew my work; I'd taken one of her memoir seminars. It made me wonder if all the heartfelt support and encouragement for what she called my *gifts* had been some kind of cruel prank. Or was *We all know Jamie Rose can't write* something that she said in a fit of jealousy . . . We're all human, right? But when I thought about it, you know, those classes she taught weren't free—had she duplicitously taken my money? You can see where this kind of spiral thinking leads. Madame X grinned, sharpening her talons. MXs proclamations about my lack of talent didn't only exist in my head but were echoed in the real world.

After I got the book deal, each time I sat down to write, instead of compulsively typing *All work and no play makes Jack a dull boy* like Jack Nicholson's berserk character in *The Shining,* my head spun with *we all know Jamie Rose can't write we all know Jamie Rose can't write Jamie Rose can't write can't write can't write!* It was brutal, but day by day, word by word, graph by graph, I did it. I used the fuck out of Cosmic Rage.

My goal became not to write a good book but to win the war against Madame X.

When I turned in the manuscript, I was convinced my publisher would tell me the book stunk—that she'd give a big Jamie Rose-can't-write hyena laugh and ask me to return my advance. What she *did* say was that it was the first self-help book that made her cry. I shakily said, "Cry good? Or cry bad?" She knew what I meant and said, "Cry good."

The book became a bestseller—in the Rose family. In the rest of America, not so much. But I won that battle by sending Madame X to the hell where she belongs. And you know what? This neurotic, insecure book nerd now had a title in the Library of Congress.

~

MX wants you to believe your inherent value is worthless. She wants to proclaim, YOU ARE NOT. The Cosmic Rage tool helps you claim your space in the universe so you can move into action, free from the limiting declarations of the pernicious Madame.

We are born with the cosmic right to express ourselves—

WE ARE.

The Groper

A few years ago, I went to India, to cross off a bucket-list destination—the Taj Mahal. It didn't disappoint. I had a similar feeling when I saw the majesty of the Grand Canyon for the first time. The Taj completely silenced me, shutting off my inner dialogue. Shining incandescently with reflected and otherworldly light, it invites you into its dream. I had worried that the Taj Mahal would be just another "postcard" experience, but to paraphrase the great Carrie Fisher, the palace was like a postcard from the edge of Infinity.

The entrance was through a narrow doorway choked by a tourist bottleneck. As I pressed up single file against my friends (and strangers), I heard the man behind me tell someone he was with, "I hope I don't get pushed—'cause when I'm pushed, I *grope.*" I thought, *Yuck. What a creepy thing to say.* I glanced back to see a well-dressed seventy-something man smiling at me. The line started moving again. Suddenly, a body stumbled against me and a hand grabbed my ass. I reflexively thought it was an accident—then recalled, "When I'm pushed, I *grope.*" In a cold rage, I turned, got in his face and shouted, "When I get groped, I slap!" He smiled and smugly said, "As well you should." I was on fire with rage as my group continued our journey into the Taj Mahal. None of my friends saw what had happened, nor heard my warning to the man.

I was proud of myself for speaking up, but the rage stayed with me for several hours and well into that night. I fantasized about paying money to a gang to hold him down while I grabbed whatever tiny thing he had in his pants and *twisted*. I'd whisper, "When I get pushed, I *castrate*"—while he screamed in agony. I was literally sick with anger. I needed to find a way to process my shock and fury, a way to release it in a positive way.

The following Tool was born.

THE TOOL
The Volcano
(J.R.)

Imagine you're a volcano that's lain dormant for hundreds of years. Now, begin to feel a warm, unsettled, sensation stirring in your core.

The sensation intensifies, getting stronger and hotter, becoming violent and fiery. As this force becomes more powerful, it creates fissures on your surface. The pressure builds and the fissures burst open in an explosion of blazing lava. The lava spills out onto the land around you, enveloping it in thick, red-hot molten rock.

Continue to feel the raging force of the lava expel from your core until, eventually, you feel it is fully released.

The pressure is gone. You feel calmer now.

Gradually you sense a shift in temperature—a cool feeling washes over you, soothing any fiery activated areas left inside. You're once again in a quiet, dormant state.

The lava covering the land around you also cools, and as it does, it releases elements into the earth, like magnesium and potassium, making the soil fertile.

You feel relaxed and profoundly serene. You know that you always have the potential to unleash this powerful force—and you know also that it's a positive, necessary part of life.

~

Some of my clients have had trouble giving themselves permission to access anger. The Volcano Tool helps them to feel the value of this essential emotion. It also provides a way to release pent-up anger so it doesn't fester inside. Remember, just as fire can be used to provide warmth and light, it can also destroy. What leveled two favorite cities of mine—Pacific Palisades and Altadena—also cooks our food and cauterizes wounds.

Like fire, the force of anger isn't inherently negative. It depends on how it's used.

An X-Takeover

I was seven years old and had just become a Brownie. So exciting! Mom bought me a Brownie dress, and I couldn't wait to show it off at school.

I've always been sensitive to textures and temperatures. I still am—wool—even cashmere, makes my skin crawl. I had a habit of warming my clothes before putting them on, something that my mother wasn't aware of. We had a small Thermador heater in the wall of the bathroom of our little apartment. In the cold mornings, before getting dressed for school, I hung my undershirts and tops over the caged grille that covered the coils until my clothes were nice and toasty. That morning, I did just that with my uniform and went to the kitchen for cereal. I dawdled a bit with my Lucky Charms and by the time I went back for the dress, it was *smoking.* "Mom!" I cried. She ran in and instantly grabbed the dress, which was already blackened. She understood what I had done. Reta held the dress in one hand and yanked me into the kitchen. She turned on a gas burner and lit the hem of the dress on fire. As it burned, she screamed, "This is what could have happened to *you!*" —then threw the incinerated thing into the sink, doused it with water, and ran to her bedroom, slamming the door behind her.

Alone in the kitchen, I could hear her sobbing.

I was frightened and confused. What had I just seen? Was she trying to protect me or kill me? It was like watching a scary movie—a gorgon, holding my Brownie dress over her head like a fiery weapon. My mother had been overtaken by Madame X.

When Madame X is controlling someone, that person is in an inflamed state. This can last for a few moments, or, in a person more susceptible, it can become a permanent condition. MX is a force that isn't subject to logic and reason; everyone and everything is a threat. When someone's in this state, *reason* is as effective as feathers against fire. Years later, after my mother got sober, I asked her about the infamous day that she burned the Brownie dress. She burst into tears; obviously, it was a memory she buried long ago. "I'm so sorry I scared you! I didn't know how to handle things—*anything*—back then. I was overwhelmed. I worked all day, your father was out of town so much, and you were being taken care of by babysitters. They were so unreliable . . . I felt terrible about leaving you with them all the time but didn't have a choice. I was *out of my mind* when I saw that dress—especially when I realized you'd put it on the heater so many times before. What if I hadn't been home? What if you had set the apartment on fire and burned yourself alive!"

My client Nina's boyfriend, Henry, had just moved in. Both were fresh out of unhappy, long-term marriages and waited a long time before making the decision to try again. Nina and Henry were uncommonly compatible and rarely argued. Two weeks into their new living arrangement, Henry went grocery shopping, something Nina usually did, but she was busy with work and he wanted to help out. She was delighted. As she unpacked the groceries, she saw that he'd bought coffee beans. Without rancor, she said, "Oh, you got beans. We use ground." Clearly upset, Henry shouted, "I wanted to do something for you and all you have to say is that I bought *beans* instead of fucking *ground*?" Nina was startled. She didn't mean the comment as a condemnation. Still, she apologized.

"You're absolutely right. I *so* appreciate you going shopping. I should have said that first thing." In spite of her trying to soothe things over, his anger escalated. "I don't know how to grocery shop, okay? I'm a fucking broker! That's all I know how to do!"

It only took a moment for Henry to go from zero to two hundred miles an hour; Nina mirrored him by blurting out, "Look—it was *your* idea to move in. If you're so *pissed* about such a tiny little thing, you can find another place!"

He stormed out, slamming the door behind him. Nina was shaken and upset. They'd never had a fight like this. It felt like her first marriage all over again. One of the reasons she'd divorced her ex was because of the constant bickering—she didn't want to relive that nightmare.

Nina happened to have a session booked with me the next morning. When she told me the story, I knew exactly what had happened. Part X had taken over them both; one had triggered the other, causing an X-plosion. When a person has an extreme reaction, it's usually an indicator that they're afraid of something—like Mom was when she did her dance of fire with my Brownie dress—or reacting to an old, unrelated event. Fear often makes one lose touch with the *present*, making it easy to get flung into distant or imagined fears. (In twelve-step programs, there's the expression, "If it's hysterical, it's historical.") In this frightened, agitated state, it's easy to become overtaken by X.

If two people are consumed by the X force, they enter a labyrinth of bitterness and hostility. I reminded Nina that Madame X hates forward motion.

"She hates joy—but most of all, she hates *love.* Henry was in the middle of an X-takeover. When you're in the presence of a person who is experiencing that, the worst thing you can do is respond in kind. If you do, you both become trapped in what Stutz calls the Maze—a toxic loop. Unless you want a repeat of your last marriage, you have to detach yourself emotionally. But not just detach, detach with love."

Together, we did the following Tool.

THE TOOL
X-posure
(P.S.)

The moment you realize a person has been taken over, imagine a RED X *hovering above their head. The X is red because it's enflamed.*

Now, imagine a ball of white light above your own head. This light has a cooling, soothing quality.

Imagine sending this cooling light from above your head to the RED X *above the other person's head.*

The Tool is called X-posure because you're literally being exposed to a person overtaken by the X force. This Tool may or may not cool the other person down, but you know who it will cool down? *You.*

~

Relationships are a breeding ground for Madame X. This also makes them a huge opportunity for growth. Relationships are *spiritual training*; they bring out our best tendencies—and our worst. We can experience the joy of connection but can also be triggered in a way that ignites the most primitive, base parts of ourselves. Usually when couples fight, they're afraid of something. That fear often presents as anger.

The idea isn't to allow yourself to be mistreated. But detaching *with love* will bring you to a solid, spiritually connected state. From there, you can choose how to respond, not react.

Henry went to a hotel that night and Nina was distraught. After our session, she saw that he had left an embarrassed, apologetic voicemail. When she came home, he was sitting in a chair in front of the building with a huge bouquet of flowers. Now, both of them work the Tools that I've shared with Nina in our sessions. They've been together for three years and rarely get stuck in the Maze.

When they do, the Tools show them the way out.

The use of *X-posure* isn't limited to people with whom you're in a close relationship. You may snap at a barista or have to deal with a surly customer service rep. Madame X wants you to go from zero to two hundred—while strangers film it on their phones—but if you do, and MX gets her way, you've entered the Maze. Not meeting anger with anger may seem like a small thing.

There are no small things.

Chapter Three
The Mother

> She is so bright and glorious that you cannot look at her face or her garments for the splendor with which she shines. For she is terrible with the terror of the avenging lightning, and gentle with the goodness of the bright sun.
>
> —Hildegard von Bingen

> Mother is the first manifestation of power . . . and that manifestation is always feminine. I have seen many worshipers of the Divine Mother. They are all great men.
>
> —Swami Vivekananda

The Mother archetype is the strongest force in the universe. She is the Divine Feminine, the creator of all things, the force of life itself. Mythologically, she is known as Durga, Gaia, Yemaya, Isis, Demeter. In Jewish mysticism, she is the angel who whispers to each blade of grass:

Grow.

The Mother's goal is to nurture and unify all humanity. She manifests herself in our individual lives as confidence, serenity, optimism, and forward-moving energy. When we are connected to her, we feel a sense of flow. We experience synchronicity and happy coincidences. Things seem to go our way.

Before we go any further, I want you to connect with this primal, benevolent force. I want you to create your own image of the archetypal Mother. Remember, this is not your actual human mother, but an image that, for you, represents the essence of the ultimate Mother energetic.

EXERCISE

Close your eyes and visualize the Mother force. Give her some kind of form.

For some, she may look like a religious figure—Mother Mary or Eve. For others, the Hindu goddess Lakshmi, the African Yemaya, or Oshun. You might see her as a painting: Botticelli's The Birth of Venus, *a Georgia O'Keeffe flower, or one of Hilma af Klint's theosophical, abstract works. Mother might be the ocean during a storm, a multi-petaled lotus blossom, a dark sky lit with stars.*

If you aren't visually inclined, you can experience her as the scent of gardenia or rosemary or freshly baked bread. The Mother can surround you like a magnificent piece of music: Ralph Vaughan Williams's "The Lark Ascending" or Nina Simone's recording of "Wild Is the Wind."

It doesn't matter how literal or nonliteral the image is, what matters is that you feel *her. She is the Divine Mother, an unconditionally loving, benevolent, life-giving presence.*

~

Some of my clients have a hard time with this exercise because they had mothers who were critical and rejecting or verbally and physically abusive. As a result, mistrustful of women, they renounce or undervalue the feminine. But the Divine Mother energetic has *nothing* to do with our actual human mothers. All women, whether or not they've given birth, are inextricably connected with the Mother force.

When we reject her, we reject a part of ourselves

Mother Monster

My mother was my original Madame X.

I was born in New York City. Dad was a singer and Mom was a dancer, so they mostly worked at night. My brother Stevie was two years younger than me. We had babysitters whenever they were doing shows but during the day, Mom took care of us in our small apartment on Columbus Avenue. While Stevie slept, I had her all to myself. She'd cook my favorite food, "egg soup" (soft-boiled eggs) and goof around, teaching me dances and songs from her shows. She'd shuffle-step and twirl and do what she called belly-busters—the high kicks she did as a Radio City Music Hall Rockette. I tried earnestly to imitate her moves, spinning until I was dizzy, awkwardly kicking my little legs up like a can-can girl duckling following its mom. When I was sufficiently exhausted, we'd nap together (I was always the little spoon). While petting me and smoothing my hair, she'd sing "You are my sunshine, my only sunshine" or "I love you a bushel and a peck, a bushel and a peck and a hug around the neck." I loved her smell, her touch, her voice—I couldn't get enough of her. I always wanted more.

Sometimes, Mom left Stevie at home with the babysitter and brought me with her to work at a variety club called the Latin Quarter. Clubs like that don't exist anymore. They were an offshoot of vaudeville and burlesque and hosted variety acts (think Ricky Ricardo's Tropicana Club from *I Love Lucy*.) The performers included singers, contortionists, dancing dogs, comedians, and acrobats, interspersed with dance numbers performed by the beautiful Latin Quarter girls—including real dancers like my mom—sweating out time-steps, chaîne turns, fan-kicks and pirouettes. Showgirls, with their tasseled pasties, G-strings, and elaborate headdresses, strutted elegantly around the stage like preening peacocks.

Their dressing room was my playpen—a bustling, magical world of fishnets and fringe, sequins and feathers, tulle and lipstick, and legs and hips and boobs, all smelling of sweat, Max Factor pancake, Aqua Net hairspray and Jean Naté cologne. I was mesmerized: gorgeous women hooking corsets around their already slim torsos and strapping tap shoes onto high-arched feet while they hurried to make their entrances. When Mom was onstage, I got love-bombed with tickles and kisses, Cracker Jacks and ice cream.

Sometimes one of the gals held me in her arms so I could watch the show from the wings. The stage lights created a glittering tropical storm as the Latin Quarter girls danced through the electric showers and there'd be my mother, easy to spot with her bright red hair. For me, she was the prettiest Latin Quarter girl of all—my shimmering jewelry box ballerina.

During intermissions, Mom played a game with me. She'd put her hand on her forehead then slowly moved it down her face. As it dropped down, her expression changed. When the hand passed over her eyes, they closed; when it passed over her coral-painted lips, it turned the corners of her mouth from a smile to a grimace. Then she paused, her face now set in a cruel mask. It scared me. I would burn with suspense, impatient for her to change back—would she this time? Sometimes I'd try to push her hand back up her face, but she made me wait. That was part of the game. Finally, she'd slowly move her hand up, transforming back into my beautiful loving mommy. The game delighted me, "Again! Again!" I'd cry.

I couldn't know it then, but this game was a whisper from the future.

I was around ten when the drinking started. By then we'd moved to Los Angeles and Mom started selling real estate. Dad's acting career wasn't going well and he began spending most of each month in Fresno (two hundred miles north of LA) selling home improvement products for his uncle. Mom was at the office all day and often had to present offers in the evenings. My brother and I became "latchkey" kids—there was no one offering us milk and cookies when we got home from school; no one asking how our day was; no one encouraging us to do our homework. We'd make our own evening meals, cans of Chef Boyardee spaghetti or Swanson frozen TV dinners, then watch TV until Mom staggered in. Sometimes that wasn't until midnight, but until she got home, neither of us could sleep. We'd wait by the window until her headlights burned through the curtains. Once we knew she was *still alive*,

Stevie went to bed and pretended he was asleep so he wouldn't have to deal—he didn't want to see the mommy-monster. I dealt with it in a different way; I confronted her. "Where have you been?" I'd yell, "You're drunk! You're disgusting!" Most of the time our fights ended with her slapping me, slurring "Get to bed!" But I got what I wanted: Attention. Even negative attention was better than nothing.

I was born with an hemangioma, a scary name for the strawberry birthmark on my throat. But the hemangioma was growing. It appeared as a discolored lump on the surface of the skin, but like an iceberg, had mass below. The doctor's concern was that its unchecked growth could be fatal. When I was around one and a half years old, the treatments began. The first was dry ice. No anesthesia. I have a dim memory of this—I'm screaming but there's no containment for my scream. My scream travels through outer space, through the dark, still, silent universe, into infinity. When Mom would slap me in those drunken nights, I felt my scream was finally heard.

Mom drank all through my teens. One night, my best friend LeeAnn was over and I asked if I could spend the night at her house. Reta was wasted but insisted on driving, even though LeeAnn's house was only a few blocks away. "I want to make sure her parents are home," she snarled, as if suddenly she was Mother of the Fucking Year. Her hands gripped the steering wheel; her jaw locked in the hard grimace she got when she was about to snap. LeeAnn was in the back seat. I was riding shotgun. Mom made us put our seat belts on, but *she* was the danger behind the wheel. It wasn't other drivers I feared but the sudden strike of her fist. Each unexpected time, it still came as a shock—the sting of the slap, the fist on the jaw. Riding that line of Mom's rage became a game; dancing on the edge was dangerous but morbidly thrilling. *How far can I push this sloppy, ugly drunk?* And the worst part is that she was *haughty*. With mascara running and a belly bulging under her zip-up velour robe, she was still "better" than everyone else—and let you know it through slurred speech.

When she began one of her veiled, better-than-them spiels, I rolled my eyes at LeeAnn, who couldn't help but giggle. Mom caught all of it and shouted "Hey! What's going on?" "*Nothing*, Mom—" It was *so* embarrassing. I was relieved when she let it go and stared straight ahead again, gripping the wheel like a deranged race car driver. *How the hell does she manage to drive so well when she's plastered?* I used to wish her drunkenness made her weave so she'd get pulled over—her face splashed across the local paper.

Handcuffs would be the icing on the cake.

Reta squeezed the steering wheel so hard that her finger bones burned white. By then, LeeAnn and I were exchanging mischievous glances. Hyperaware Mom sinisterly uttered, "Something's not kosher in Disneyland." What the *hell*—what does that even *mean*! LeeAnn and I can't hold it in any longer and burst out laughing.

I'm riding the line big-time now, sharing this moment with my half-frightened friend, savoring our closeness, but loving that my b.f. is *seeing* this . . . I'm not alone! Mom looks like she's going to pull that steering wheel right off.

At LeeAnn's house (it seemed like it took a week to get there), she parks the car, wheels scraping against the curb like chalk on a blackboard. When I struggle to open the door, Mom gives me a look of abject hatred. I can feel the force of it. I steal another glance at LeeAnn.

"I want to make sure her parents are home," Mom slurs, cocky and all-knowing, like we're two little con women. Can't pull the wool over her eyes!

Those days, I used to fantasize about killing her. I longed to scrape my nails down her smug, alcoholic face. As a child, my mother was battered, so her instincts toward cruelty were always there, long before she started seriously drinking. She used to tell "funny" anecdotes from when I was a baby. "You were in your high chair and I was feeding you a soft-boiled egg—egg soup we called it—your favorite. You were playing and kept spitting it out at me . . . oh, you were laughing! You thought it was *so* funny. So, you know what I did? I dumped that bowl of egg on *right on your head*. Well, *that* stopped you." I feel as though I can remember the shock of the warm mucousy egg dripping down my cheeks. Later, at eight years old, I was messing around at dinner, cracking jokes with my cousins. Suddenly, Mom flipped over a plate of spaghetti on my head.

At LeeAnn's door, Mom rings the bell. Before it opens, Mom whips her face toward me, lips pressed together—that look of pure hatred again—and slaps me hard across my face. Just in time not to see it, LeeAnn's mother greets us. "Hello!" My face stings and I'm seeing stars. I stare at the woman like a deer in the headlights. Mom says, "Hi! Oh, good, you're home! I wanted to make sure." She waddles back to her car. I follow my horrified friend inside.

How do you unlearn hatred? How do you unravel its dark threads, the ones you wove for protection?

In order to survive, I had to learn to hate the thing I most loved, to renounce the need for the thing—the person—I needed most.

~

Reta quit drinking in 1981 (I was twenty-one), and I stopped the next year. I was lucky to get sober young. I didn't fit the profile of the people I met who got sober when I did—I never had a DUI, never had a blackout, but preferred to drink alone, and always for the effect. When I did drink socially, I started having a personality change—I got angry and slovenly, just like Mom—for me, a fate worse than death. Reta's mother, my Grandma Ellen, died from alcoholism at forty-seven. I knew that if I kept on that path, I'd end up dead. Or even worse, alive—and a practicing alcoholic.

The visceral hatred for my mother stayed with me long after both she and I were sober. She'd done her best to make amends, apologizing so many times over the years for the way she'd treated me growing up. I listened and reassured her that I forgave her, even though I still had resentment in my heart. By my forties, my hatred had simmered down to a tolerable annoyance. But my affection for her was skin-deep. I was okay with that; it was enough just not to hate her.

When I left my husband and moved next door to my parents—I was fifty-four—life decided to bring me closer not just logistically but emotionally. Dad was diagnosed with

Alzheimer's by then and I'd take him to lunch and doctor appointments while Mom oversaw the copious amount of work necessary for his care. I was shocked to see how bad things had gotten. Dad couldn't be left alone, couldn't feed himself, and had to be reminded to undress before showering. "I take my clothes off first, right?" It would have been funny if it wasn't so heartbreaking. Even though he wore adult diapers, he still wet his bed almost every night, so Mom was always doing laundry. Doling out and organizing his weekly pills took more than half an hour.

Watching the way she took care of my father, her selfless devotion, I felt such respect. As Dad's disease progressed, slipping him farther and farther away from us, I grew closer to my mother. I started to really like her. Even though she was worked to the bone taking care of Stewart, she showed up at my apartment door with home-baked pies and cookies, and little presents she found for me at her favorite stores, Marshall's and Home Goods.

One day I asked myself, do I want a "justified" resentment? Or do I want a mother?

One night, in the terrible weeks before he died, we were (yet again) with Dad in the ER. There was a curtain around his hospital bed. Mom and I were just outside it while a doctor and some nurses were trying to put a catheter in. My father was screaming, "No! It hurts! It hurts me!" and crying like a child. It was unbearable to know that he didn't understand what was happening to him—I was helpless and had no way to soothe his fear. My face was buried in my hands and I was silently weeping when I felt arms wrap around me—my mother's. I let her hold me. It was the first time since I was a little girl that I didn't want to pull away.

A few weeks later, Dad was gone.

Until then, I felt that I had reached the ceiling of forgiveness with my mother. That we were close *enough*. But life had other plans.

Daughterhood

After my father died, Mom was at sea. They'd been married over fifty years and for the last five or so, her whole life was about taking care of him. With Stewart gone, there was a tremendous void. She lost her sense of purpose. She shared with me the pain of her new "firsts"—ticking *Widowed* on medical forms; shopping and cooking for one. Sharing dinner in her apartment, we'd make small talk, but when there was a pause, she'd smile sorrowfully and say, "I miss him." I would touch her hand; she knew how much I missed him too. "He was sick, but at least I had a husband." They had been Reta and Stewart since she was nineteen but now, at nearly eighty, the two were no more. In that dinnertime moment of helplessness, I asked myself what I could do to help her.

The answer came: *Let her be my mother.*

We began spending lots of time together. I took her to plays and restaurants. We became series regulars at her beloved discount shopping outlets and costarred at Costco.

Growing up, the holidays were always a big deal in our family. We showered each other with gifts. It was easier to express our love that way than it would have been with tenderness. Even though we were Jewish (Mom converted from

Mormonism), in addition to our menorah, we dyed Easter eggs and put up a Christmas tree. You can take the girl out of the church but you can't take the church out of the girl. Mom was a great cook and made best-in-show caramel corn, pecan pies, the most succulent turkey and stuffing, and even potato latkes.

After Dad's passing, I tried bringing some of that magic back. Our neighborhood went all out during the holidays and I took Mom on walks to see the Christmas lights and Halloween decorations. When she grew frail, we took the car and visited other neighborhoods, famous for their over-the-top decorative extravaganzas. A few Halloweens ago, when even getting in and out of the car became a hardship for her, I had a brainstorm to set up a trick-or-treat station outside our building. We sat in two lawn chairs on the sidewalk, with big buckets of candy. In our funny hats and light-up pumpkin earrings, we cooed over the kids' costumes as they obliviously gorged on our sugar bombs. Mom was gleeful and said, "If I'm alive next year let's do this again!"

That was our last holiday together.

Reta had been having symptoms for months—pain, incontinence—but kept getting diagnosed with UTIs. One doctor tried an in-office cystoscopy to look at the urethra and bladder, a procedure he had to abandon because of the excruciating pain it caused her. He saw enough to tell her that she had a severe vaginal prolapse and needed to see a specialist. Easier said than done. Specialists were booked months in advance; without a connection, getting an appointment was next to impossible. We went through a weekly revolving ER door but the only diagnosis we ever got was the token UTI. She was in agony; all she came home with was extra-strength Tylenol and useless antibiotics. Her symptoms worsened—there were huge blood clots in her urine. Still, she soldiered on. She even joined a local senior center where she quickly became a Texas Hold'em champion. Finally, she was in too much discomfort to leave her apartment. One morning, I went over to her place and she looked like she'd been crying—very unusual for her customarily stoic demeaner. "Look," she said and took me into her bathroom. The tub was filled with soaked diapers. "This is all from last night." She wasn't sleeping at all. She tried to get used to wetting herself while she slept but couldn't. "Jamie, I don't want to live like this."

Our appointment with the specialist was weeks away. We finally got a prescription for pain pills but because of the hoopla around opiates, doctors would only write them for five at a time. I was desperate enough to start calling friends to see if they had any expired Vicodin laying around that they could spare. Like Mom's journey with my father, taking care of her became the focus of my life. I spent hours networking to find a physician who could see her sooner. I made sure she ate and stayed hydrated. A nightmare of helplessness overwhelmed me. The months of stress were taking a toll. One day, I felt a wetness in my underwear. I went to the bathroom and although I'd been in menopause for ten years, I was bleeding.

I was literally bleeding stress.

Finally, I got a spot with a specialist at USC. After looking through months of test results and CT scans, he immediately ordered a cystoscopy under anesthesia. We were finally going to get some answers.

The night before the procedure I wrote in my journal,

> *March 7, 2024— . . . I wonder what will be discovered in this operation? What future there is for her? I want her to go out happy. God, please let me be with her when she passes. Let me be able to make her feel safe and loved . . .*

The morning of the cystoscopy, Mom was so happy.

"I get to sleep!"

They let me stay with her in the pre-op cubicle. I hadn't seen her so content in months.

"I get to be put *out*," she laughed. "I've never looked so forward to a procedure!"

When a nurse came in and began catheterizing her, Mom screamed like she was being butchered. "It hurts! It hurts!" She squirmed and gulped for air.

"I was supposed to be *sedated*! I was supposed to be *asleep*!"

The nurse panicked. "It's just fluid—so they can see inside—"

"She was supposed to be out for this!" I shouted, boiling with rage. "*Get her pain medicine*—NOW!"

"But the doctor has to order—"

"Then *get the doctor*," I bellowed.

She ran out.

Mom's eyes beseeched me, begging for help, "*Jamie, I can't stand it, I can't stand it*—" I was in agony but needed to stay strong so I could take care of her, protect her. I wrapped her in my arms and stroked her forehead, trying somehow to soothe her. "I'm here, Mommy . . . just *breathe*, Sweetheart. They're getting you medicine for the pain." All she could do was sob;

she was broken. I felt the same as I did when my Dad was being catheterized in the ER—that sense of horror and helplessness—but this time, I had my arms around my mother, instead of her arms around me. Now, I was trying to contain *her* misery, holding her as if she were my own child. I never wanted to let go.

Finally, the nurse returned with IV pain meds. Moments later, Mom passed out. I went to the waiting room. When the doctor came to talk to me, the look on his face was bad news: Stage 4 bladder cancer. He told us it had been there for months and was incredulous the cancer had gone undiagnosed. He said that it was "somewhat" treatable with immunotherapy, and not an immediate death sentence. *How comforting.* We made an appointment to see him the following week.

The next morning at 6 a.m., my boyfriend woke me up. "It's your mom. The paramedics are here. Be prepared—there's shit everywhere."

I didn't know what he meant.

I ran down the hall to her apartment. The front door was open and the stench hit me first. Her bedroom floor was smeared with feces. Mom sat on the edge of her bed, nude, a towel draped over her. Three paramedics stood around her. There was excrement on her legs, feet, arms. The feeling of sadness in the room was palpable; one of the EMTs had tears in his eyes. (He later took me aside and said that he had an elderly mother too.) I tried to comfort Mom as she sat there, crumpled and defeated, her head down, humiliated and ashamed. "It's okay, Mommy. It's just human stuff." One of the men murmured in agreement, "Yes, just human." She was breaking our hearts. She said that she woke up with diarrhea and tried to get to the bathroom but didn't make it. The stool ran down her legs onto the floor, where she slipped and fell. That's why it was all over her body.

She called 911 because she didn't want to wake me.

When the paramedics left, I cleaned Mom and sat her in the living room while I mopped the floor and changed the bedding. Thankfully, the doctor had sent her home with pain pills, so she was able to sleep. She never recovered from that day.

A week later, Mom and the family—my brother and sister-in-law, Mom, and me—had a telehealth call with the doctor. Shocked at how weakened she'd become, he said that she was no longer a candidate for treatment. Mom politely listened, then said, "I want a pleasant death."

We began home hospice.

I was so grateful to be living next door. I'd go over there around 7 a.m., feed her cats and clean the litter, then empty her urine bag and dispense her morning meds. I made coffee and prodded her to eat a little cereal or toast. When she was ready, I helped her walk to the living room where she'd read or watch television. I finally understood the phrase "borrowed time," and it hurt. One day—soon—she wouldn't be here when I went through that door.

For the first week or so of hospice, she was fine on her own during the day. Since I worked at home, writing and doing sessions online, I was right there if she needed me. Medicare sent nurses every few days to check her vitals and order meds. One day, an RN and I were giving Mom a sponge bath in bed. In that moment, I felt such tenderness toward her. I guess it showed in my face because the nurse quietly said, "I understand. I lost my mother thirteen years ago." I asked if she was with her mom when she passed. She said no—she was living in another country. "I love my job," she said. "When I am helping them, I see my own mother."

When it got to the point where she needed a full-time caregiver during the day, we hired a lady who got there in the morning and left after making Mom dinner. Then I took over and hung out until she went to sleep. I'd go back to my place for the night. She had strict orders to call *immediately* if she needed me. (I didn't want a repeat of that terrible 911 morning.) I'd come over early to prepare her for the day, and the caregiver's arrival. Those mornings and evenings with my mother are some of my most precious memories. "What a pretty face to wake up to," she'd say when I stepped into the bedroom. We talked about everything, even about what to put on her headstone—at her request.

"How about this?" I offered. "'Wife. Mother. Grandmother. Rockette.'"

"Yes!" she practically squealed. "Rockette! With two T's!"

Journal entry:

April 4th 2024—This morning Mom greeted me with "Good morning Cinderella!" So sweet. I'd gone to a party with Bruce at LACMA the night before (for the Ed Ruscha show). I told her about the event, kind of pumped it up to make it fun for her, told her which celebrities were there (Jane Fonda!) I'd showed her my outfit before I left. Our family has always loved dressing up. "Did you receive compliments?" she asked. "Yes!" It made her so happy. I was getting sleepy—hadn't slept well—kept yawning. She said, "Why don't you go back to your apartment?" I said no, I want to stay here with you. "Then why don't you get in bed with me?" Her hospital bed—a twin. I did. She hugged me from the back . . . spooning, "You're my baby. You and I used to lay like this when you were little. It was so sweet." She stroked my arms, my hair. "You were my little baby. Then you were my little girl. Then you were my teenager and I was so rough on you. You had it so tough." I could hear that she was crying softly. I patted her hand. "None of that matters anymore Mom. You've more than made up for it. I love you so much." Then I was crying too. It was so tender. I remember feeling like I did when I was little. Before the drinking. Before everything.

She got weaker. She was barely eating. She had trouble swallowing and took eyedroppers of morphine for the pain. Each morning, on my way down the hall to her apartment, I wondered if I would find her dead in her bed.

It was time to hire a caretaker for the night shift.

The medicine was starting to affect her. One morning, she whispered in my ear, "'*Don't panic.*' I keep hearing that. Do you? Do you hear it? 'Don't Panic'—?"

"No, Mom, I don't."

Then she pulled away, her expression changing to one of harsh contempt. "You're *doing* something to me, aren't you?" She was paranoid—but in that moment, I went straight back to that night with LeeAnn and the absurd, infamous, "Something's not kosher in Disneyland . . . " I went straight back to the Slap. For a moment, the monster was back.

That morning, around 3 a.m., I got a frantic call from Maria, the night caregiver.

"Please come! She's acting crazy!"

When I rushed over, Maria met me at the door, totally freaked out. "Your mother is screaming out the window!"

When I entered the bedroom, Mom was wild-eyed. "Help! Help me, Jamie! I'm killing them! I'm killing the whole building! The line, the line!—" She grabbed at her catheter. "I'm poisoning them! I'm killing them with the line! Call 911!"

I tried to hold her but she moved away. "Mom, everyone's okay! We're *okay*, you're *okay* . . . "

"No!" she screamed. "I'm serious, Jamie! You have to call 911!" She grabbed at the phone and shoved it into my hands. I tried a different tack.

"I already called them, Mama, don't worry! Everything's going to be okay." Maria passed me the bottle of morphine. "Let me give you some medicine."

"*Please*," she cried. "I'm *killing* them—" I gave her the morphine and she soon calmed down. Slowly, I maneuvered her into bed. Her eyes closed and her breathing slowed. Just when I thought she was falling asleep, she said, "I think I'll be alive for one more week."

April 10th 2024— Mom in and out of consciousness now. Not eating. Tonight as she was falling asleep, I was stroking her head and gently singing to her like she did to me when I was little, "You are my sunshine, my only sunshine, You make me happy, when skies are gray." Then she joined in! We sang the last line together. "You'll *never know dear how much I love you . . ." —then she was out again. I sang the last line by myself, almost didn't get through it, "Please don't take my sunshine away . . ."*

After the night of that journal entry, she never regained consciousness.

On the morning of April 17th, my prayer was answered: I was with her as she passed. I stroked her forehead and held her thin hand, telling her how much I loved her and always will.

I felt the last flutters of her pulse and stayed with her a long time in the stillness after. It was a painful, beautiful, and sacred moment.

I loved her to death.

The Mother in Me

Madame X told me I was unqualified to write this chapter because I'm not a mother.

I was pregnant once, at seventeen. I was a senior in high school. Things were bad at home. I had an older, deadbeat boyfriend and was drinking and drugging, but my parents were so busy with their own dramas (Mom's drinking, Dad's denial) that no one seemed to care. My period was always like clockwork. When it was a week late, I knew why.

I'm not sure how I learned about the abortion place. My boyfriend gave me the money and drove me there. I remember laying draped on a table. I remember being scared. A nurse put an IV in my arm. She told me to count down from ten. As I recited the numbers, a doctor came in and stuck something inside me. Then, I was out. As I came to, a feeling of terror overtook me. I was on a bed covered in a bright white sheet, in a room with other girls on beds covered in bright white sheets. A bright white abortion factory.

I remember there was silence while the boyfriend drove me home.

I had a thick pad between my legs. I was still bleeding.

At the time, I had no feeling about the baby; none of it seemed real. But now, I wonder what that child would have become. I'll never know in this lifetime what it's like to see your belly grow fat with a baby, to give birth, to breastfeed—to send your child off to their first day of school. To go to their graduation. To be mother of the bride or groom.

But because of those last months with Reta, I know what's it's like to feel the profound connection between mother and child. To know what it's like to be both child *and* mother. With her, I experienced them both. Whether or not we've given birth, or whether we ever wanted to, the Mother force lives within us. If we renounce her, we renounce a part of ourselves. She is always available to help us.

The Mother force is the angel who whispers in our ears, *Thrive, grow, soar.*

Most women are used to giving love and support to others but are not so practiced at nurturing ourselves. In *Coming Alive,* Phil Stutz and Barry Michels wrote a wonderful Tool called the Mother. Use it when you feel demoralized—when you feel so hurt by the circumstances of your life that you feel like you can't go on.

THE TOOL
The Mother
(P.S., B.M.)
(The Sue Campbell Variation)[4]

Conjure your image of the archetypal Mother. Remember, she isn't human. She's a mystical image—the embodiment of pure, unconditional love. I see her as a combination of Botticelli's well-known painting The Birth of Venus *and a beautiful sunset.*

Now, bring up a feeling of intense demoralization and hopelessness. You feel crushed under the weight of your feelings, as if you're buried under a thick sludge. The Divine Mother appears above. She reaches down and lifts this substance off you—as she does, it disintegrates, vaporizes. Then she looks down at you with utter love and compassion—you are her precious child. She lifts you into her infinitely compassionate arms. You are safe in her loving embrace.

[4] This Tool as described differs slightly from the original version. In the original version, the Mother absorbs the pain into her body rather than vaporizes it. My client, Sue Campbell, contributed this slight difference, as an alternative to "women being expected to endlessly *absorb* pain."

Chapter Four

Shadow Dancing

I have remembered beauty in the night,
Against black silences I waked to see
A shadow stretching out with a dark plea
For some lost joy that I have forgotten quite.
—Sara Teasdale, *Flame and Shadow*

The shadow becomes hostile only when it is ignored
or misunderstood.
—Marie Louse Franz

The pioneering Swiss psychiatrist Carl Jung was the first to bring forth the idea of the shadow, describing it as "the thing a person has no wish to be." The shadow is the rejected part of ourselves—the part we want to hide from the world. Most people do everything they can to bury their shadow shelves. But as Shakespeare wrote, the truth will always out.

We see examples of this all the time: the virulently antigay religious figure caught in flagrante with a person of the same sex; the seemingly perfect social media influencer (an expert in child-rearing!) uncovered as an abuser of her own kids; the warm, funny television personality who bullies their staff; the "family man" politician who blows up his life with a sext. Yet the shadow presents itself in private controversies as well. Many of us hide our thoughts and opinions because of potential criticism. There are those who can't commit to a relationship because they're afraid of losing their independence—and creative souls who are unable to move forward with their artistic dreams because of the fear of failure.

By our early teens, most of us have pushed the shadow into the deepest parts of our subconscious. Yet, like a forgotten prisoner shut away in the bowels of a dungeon, it's still there. After years of neglect, shut out and alone, the shadow becomes distorted. Why? Because unless we have a close relationship with them, our shadows become vulnerable to attack—by Madame X. Under her pernicious influence, they express themselves in negative ways. Gentleness becomes passivity, discernment becomes judgement, sensitivity becomes self-pity. Assertiveness morphs into rage; ambition, into greed; sexuality, into sex addiction. Independence becomes isolation and moral clarity becomes self-righteousness.

Everyone I work with, regardless of how successful and confident they appear, has an insecure shadow living inside. Women share the same insecurities as men—with supersized enhancements. It's true that men can be judged by their physical attributes. But as a rule, it is women whose looks are subjected to daily, microscopic scrutiny, and shaming. As we know too well, the dominant message in society (for thousands of years) is that our value is inextricably linked to our appearance. From childhood, women are trained that their highest worth is youth and beauty. In a recent session, a client told me that her nine-year-old daughter asked for an "antiaging" red-light therapy mask she saw advertised on TikTok. (Writing that last sentence was heartbreaking.) With the ubiquity of computer-generated reimaging and retouching, things have gotten even worse. Women are bombarded by AI-enhanced images of the culture's ever-changing ideal of the "perfect" woman. If we're successful in business, we worry about not spending enough time with our kids; if we've devoted our lives to raising our children and maintaining a home, we feel we haven't achieved enough. If unable to have children—or choosing not to—we fear having missed out on an essential part of femaleness.

If you have shame about your looks, intellect, sexuality or social status and want to cultivate true confidence (and the serenity that goes along with it), it's essential that you connect with the parts of yourself you deem inferior—and *embrace* them.

Stutz breaks down the shadow into three categories: the Inferior Shadow[5], the Evil Shadow, and the Sick Shadow.[6]

EXERCISE
The Inferior Shadow

Close your eyes.

Think back to your childhood and remember a time when you felt insecure, left out, or not enough. Think about the moments you felt embarrassed or ashamed. Unprotected and scared.

[5] It's not inferior, it just feels that way.

[6] I'll talk more about the Evil Shadow and the Sick Shadow in later chapters.

Don't worry about finding the perfect example.

Maybe you're eight or ten or fourteen years old. Use whatever image comes to you.

Keeping your eyes closed, push that image out in front of you.

See that image of yourself as a separate person. A vulnerable, frightened, unprotected child.

You've just met your Inferior Shadow.

Meet My Shadow

She's eleven years old.

Standing in the schoolyard, she steels herself to endure the daily humiliation called Waiting to Be Picked for the Volleyball Team.

She has a slight disadvantage that the other girls seem not to share—*she's terrified of the ball.* All sports involving any kind of object being hurled toward her face feels like something to run *from*, not *toward.*

She's always picked last.

In a time when the pinnacle of female attractiveness is embodied by the quintessential, smooth-haired, sun-bronzed California blond, she sports frizzy red hair and pinky-white, freckly skin that she tries to darken by using a tanning product called QT. It smells like wet hay and makes her legs so orange they match her hair.

Her chest is flat but she has a woman's hips. At a pool party, she overhears a boy say, "How comes she's so small on top and so big on the bottom?"

But wait, there's more.

She's just rcceived a full set of braces along with "neck gear"—a horizontal bar affixed to her front teeth like the bumper of a car. Her one goal in life is to have a boyfriend. Specifically, a boy named David Lewis. She literally sent questionnaires to the popular girls in school, asking them to reveal their secrets. They didn't have the heart to say that her real problem was the frizzy red hair and general dorkiness. So, they repeated the advice given in magazines like *Seventeen* and *Glamour*:

Show an interest in him!

Let him know you like him!

The next morning, when she saw David Lewis, she called out, "Hi, David!" Her smile was big and bright—too bright, because of the metal grille. He turned around and burst into laughter.

"Jamie! What happened? You look like a Volkswagen!"

Now, she's twelve.

She wakes up to see brownish-reddish stains in her underwear.

The day before, she painted her nails with dark rust Biba polish; it was the same color, and she was confused. But how could it have . . . *oh my God! I got my period*! Ever since the girl's health education class earlier that year, she had been eagerly awaiting this day. She'd amassed a large collection of Kotex and also had the "sanitary belt" that was handed out in class—think of a white, unsexy, uncomfortable garter belt; this was *way* before adhesive pads were invented. Her period came on a Sunday. Monday morning, she proudly waddles into school with what feels like a submarine sandwich between her legs. Her purse is stuffed with as many extra pads as it can hold. (Because of their enormity, probably just two.)

In homeroom, she drapes her shoulder bag over the back of the chair before she sits. She's feeling *very* grown-up. Then, she hears the giggling. When she turns around, the purse is empty. The boy behind her had grabbed the napkins from her bag.

"Jamie got her period! Jamie got her period!"

He begins tossing them around the room. The boys (and some of the girls) squeal with laughter as they play hot potato with the pads while the teacher tries to intervene. Jamie sobs, "They're not mine!"—then buries her face in her hands. When Mrs. Teague finally regains control of the room, she adds to the mortification by solemnly handing the napkins back.

For the rest of class, Jamie throttles her shame and stares rigidly ahead. But she can still hear the snickers and cruel whispers.

She's fourteen.

Braces off.

She's figured out how to unkink her hair and uses mascara to darken her naturally blond eyelashes. Miraculously, she's grown modest boobs. Boys are noticing her. The mean girls who laughed on the Day of the Kotex Massacre—the ones who never picked her for the team—now find her funny and likeable. They invite her to parties.

She's popular!

All she ever wanted—

But still, she feels ashamed. Less than. Not enough.

She's sixteen.

The family's moved from LA to Fresno. Fresno feels like a backwater, an outpost of the losers and the damned. On school nights, her mother throws down glasses of vodka like a lush in a B movie. Jamie's up late, fighting with Mom—and Stevie gets caught in the friendly fire of his sister's rage. School is her only respite; she'd rather be there than at home. *Anyplace but home.* She gets good grades but smokes and drinks and does drugs to quell her shame and anxiety. After graduating high school, she moves back to LA and enrolls in college. Getting a degree isn't the reason; it's all about escape. She desperately craves independence. She hopes to somehow return to her childhood gig, acting in TV commercials.

She needs to get rich—quick.

By nineteen, she says goodbye to higher education. She has three national commercials on the air. She auditions for a night time soap and gets cast in a hit television series. *Poof,* she's a TV celebrity.

She's twenty-one.

But she's still that little girl whose self-worth was stolen. She's still being thrown around the room by a bullying world. Stardom didn't come *close* to being the antidote for the poison of self-hatred. She never drinks at the studio but counts the hours and minutes before she can go home and get drunk—alone. When she drinks around other people, she gets blowsy, angry, slurry and loud. (Instead of turning into a werewolf, she grows Rockette legs.) She avoids all that by isolating when she drinks. Alcohol is the medicine. It's the painkiller that tamps down the misery that waits in ambush. The revolving thoughts still come: *If only I can get more famous . . . if only I was prettier, thinner, more beloved by the fans . . .* maybe *then*, that feeling of less-than and not-good-enough would go away.

But she was going about it all wrong.

EXERCISE
How to Form a Relationship with Your Shadow

Close your eyes.

Bring back the image of the younger, insecure Self that you discovered at the beginning of this chapter.

Keeping your eyes closed, push that image out in front of you.

See her as a separate person—a sweet, unprotected child. Make her as vivid and as real as you can. What does her hair look like? What is she wearing? Is she sitting or standing? Where is she? At home? On the playground? Is she at school? A sleepover? Is she crying in her room?

How does she feel about herself? How does she feel about other people? How does she feel about the world?

What is happening in her life?

Now, try to make contact . . .

Simply look at her. Is she looking back at you? (Maybe she isn't.)

If she'll allow it, go and sit next to her. If that feels like too much, just stand beside her.

Can you hold her hand? Will she let you put your arm around her? She might pull away—she may not be ready for you to touch her, or even be near her. That's okay. Stay present in whatever way she'll allow.

In your own words, tell her how sorry you are for having abandoned her. Apologize for making her feel unworthy.

Tell her you've realized that she is the very best part of you—that your creativity, your uniqueness, your ability to give and receive love all come from her.

Tell her you're going to work to build a relationship with her. She may not believe you! Why should she? You've ignored her for so long . . .

She may have been poorly treated by other children—even her parents—but those days are long gone. For the last however many years, you've *been the one mistreating her. Your job is to comfort her, to love her, to make her feel safe and accepted and valued. To convince her that she isn't alone. And the only way to prove it to her is by visiting her—again and again.*

After a few minutes, thank your shadow for allowing you to spend time with her. Promise her that you'll be back soon.

Keep your promise.

~

You may find that exercise difficult.

At first, your shadow may be hazy and undefined—or just a "feeling." *That's okay.* There isn't a right way to do this exercise. You're in the early stages of your shadow courtship. If you work hard at it, I promise that the shadow will reveal more and more of herself. She will begin to trust you.

And you will begin to trust yourself.

My client, Laura, is the owner of a multimillion-dollar advertising agency. In business, she's a lioness, overseeing hundreds of employees, and invited to speaking engagements all over the world. But in her personal life, she's timid and anxious. At forty-two, she's never had a relationship that lasted longer than a few months. "At some point," she said hesitantly, "I always break it off. And always because I find something about them that's *wrong.* The real reason is that I want to break it off before they do."

I guided Laura to connect with her shadow.

She closed her eyes and saw herself at thirteen, a shy, skinny girl with a bad haircut. I asked how this little girl *felt* and Laura said, "She hates herself. She thinks she's ugly. How could anyone *like* her, let alone love her?" Laura's worst fears were realized when she got teased by a boy she had a crush on. He said, "You're kind of in the sale section of the girlfriend store.'" Something in her broke. The "sale section" walls that she put up grew higher and more fortified, right into adulthood. If she became too attached, she would need to find something "wrong"—because what guarantee would she have that she wouldn't be wounded?

But as I said at the beginning of this chapter, the truth will out. The shadow cannot be contained. Until Laura could love her childhood shadow—the one that grew up alongside her—how could the adult Laura love herself? It was *that* primal relationship that she couldn't afford to break off. I coached her to connect with the little girl who was living inside her by doing the shadow exercise religiously; to always keep that brokenhearted child in her mind's eye. I said "*Talk* to her, invite her in"—make her feel important, loved, accepted. Make her feel *seen.* It was difficult but she was diligent. Soon, she met a wonderful man and married him. Some days, she still feels like running away; when that happens, she connects with her shadow, reassuring her that she's worthy of love and doesn't have to be afraid. And that no matter what happens, Laura will never abandon her again.

After many years, they're still happily together—Laura and her husband, and Laura and her shadow.

Sometimes, doing this exercise, I see myself on the day those kids made fun of my period. My head buried in my hands, my body electrified by shame—the frizzy-haired carrot top with the Volkswagen grille. I see myself catching unfavorable looks in the long hall of mirrors (some from others, some from myself) that led to the rooms I sought refuge in to drink alone.

When I first tried talking with her, my inferior shadow wouldn't speak.

She hid her face from the world just as I did in the classroom. As in the exercise, I imagine myself sitting down and telling her how sorry I am for ignoring her all those years. I tell her that she has nothing to be ashamed of because she's uniquely *herself*—that's what makes her beautiful and special. I tell her that physical beauty changes, for everyone, and that the inconsistent standards of so-called beauty are bullshit; at my age, I've lived through "heroin chic" *and* the glories of big backsides. I tell her how women become perverted by the obsession of looking beautiful at all costs, and how even those who are famous for their looks disfigure themselves with too much plastic surgery or diet drugs. I tell her that I am what she will become—a woman who has learned that beauty is spirit, not body.

I tell her that she is the best of me.

The *best* of me.

After a while, she let me touch her hand. Soon, she was able to look at me. One day, she let me hold her—and she cried in my arms.

In chapter 3, I spoke of Reta dumping a bowl of egg soup on my head when I sat in my high chair, a punishment that became normalized. Throughout childhood, if I misbehaved in some way at mealtime, I literally got dumped on. Eventually, I stopped acting out but my playfulness was replaced by shame. When you've been doing shadow work a while, *other* shadows will feel safe enough to reveal themselves. I remember when a younger Shadow appeared. She looked like me, at five years old—but a monstrous version. She wore a bowl on her head and her fingernails looked like claws. When I approached, she wasn't having it. She snarled, hissing like a feral cat. But I kept showing up. "You don't have to do anything or be anything. I'm going to love you and I'm going to stay. No matter what." One day, the talons disappeared. Her hands were like the hands of a little girl again. The bowl went away too, revealing a soft halo of golden red curls. From then on, she clung to me.

Whenever I feel afraid or insecure, I go to her. I make *her* feel loved, I make *her* feel safe. I make *her* feel that she's not alone. And she does the same for me.

~

> I now see how owning our story and loving ourselves through that process is the bravest thing that we will ever do.
>
> —Brené Brown

I've never met anyone who hasn't experienced some kind of childhood trauma. I have clients whose parents and siblings were physically abusive. Some of them have family members who died by suicide or disease; many of them were tormented, not only by adults, but other children.

As you continue on your journey, long-buried memories will rise to the surface. Through the process of shadow work, some trauma can be healed. You'll find that you can rescue that damaged child and give her the love and support that she needs.

The past will merge with the present, where the healing can begin.

The shadow we've just met—the Inferior Shadow—is the one that blossomed into a stunted flower of self-hatred, watered by the random (sometimes not-so-random) cruelties that come with being alive. It's the shadow that feels less-than and not-enough. This shadow is usually the first to show its face. But other shadows must be brought into the light. We need to form relationships with them as well.

I mentioned earlier that Stutz made his own variations on the original shadow work, breaking down Jung's singular definition into three categories: the Inferior Shadow, the Evil Shadow, and the Sick Shadow. In the next chapter, we'll explore the Evil Shadow. Sometimes I think that if the Evil Shadow spoke, it might protest being given that name.

I can hear it saying the same thing Jessica Rabbit did in *Who Framed Roger Rabbit*: "I'm not bad, I'm just drawn that way."

Chapter Five

The Evil Shadow

When I'm assertive, I'm a bitch. When a man is assertive, he's a boss. He's bossed up. No negative connotation behind it. But I'm a bitch. So that's what I learned: You've got to be a bitch. Because I've never met a man in this industry that wasn't.
—Nicki Minaj

When I'm good, I'm very, very good—
but when I'm bad, I'm better.
—Mae West

I've talked about the movie *Carrie,* where a shy, bullied high school girl taps into a vital, animalistic power; if Carrie had been connected to it, that power could have been the driving force toward independence and personal expression. But without that *connection,* its potency expressed itself as ugly, demonic, and ultimately fatal. Carrie unleashes her Evil Shadow—and its vengeance showed no mercy.

Not only have women been taught to disconnect from their Evil Shadow, they've been socialized to be fearful of it. In fairy tales, that shadow is often depicted as the cruel stepmother, the wicked witch, or the repulsive old crone, living alone in the woods. In the contemporary workplace or social network, those tropes are replaced by the jealous bitch, the nasty bitch, and the ugly old bitch. But the Evil Shadow becomes a negative presence *only* when she is ignored or suppressed. When integrated, she's ferociously creative and uninhibited—and *necessary*. She colors outside the lines. She is the innovator and the one who dares; hence, she is among our most important allies. Her wildness, passion, enthusiasm and strength allow us to demand a raise, set boundaries for our children, and pursue joy. Even when others don't understand or approve.

She's the one who says NO.

Women are raised to be hypersensitive to the reactions of others—from an early age, we're assiduously coached to be "nice" at all costs. We don't want to hurt anyone's feelings, do we? Gavin de Becker has said that in our culture, "When a man says no, it's the end of a discussion. But when a woman says no, it's the beginning of a negotiation." In his book, *The Gift of Fear*, de Becker tells a story of a woman who was struggling with her groceries outside her apartment building. Despite her refusals, a helpful stranger insisted on helping her carry them inside. Once inside, he held her captive for hours. He raped her. The story illustrates how indoctrinated politeness and passivity can yield devastating consequences.

De Becker has a great acronym for the word, BITCH—"Boys I'm taking control here."

One of my earliest bad girl memories is taking a bath with my little brother when I was four years old. A massive yellow bar of Dial soap was on the side of the tub. I handed it to Stevie and said, "It's cheese. Try it!" He immediately took a big bite; he still trusted his older sis, something that would change in later years. He spat out a mouthful and cried—while I snickered. *Yes*, it was mischievous. *Yes*, one could cxcusc it as typical mean girl/big sister bullshit. But now I see that those sort of subversive actions—both large and small, extending into adulthood—were glimmers of my Evil Shadow.

~

In the following exercise, you will meet your Evil Shadow. (Sometimes I call her the *Entitled* shadow, or the *Wild* shadow. Use whatever name is most resonant for you.) You'll be asked to remember a time you did something *bad*. To jog your memory, here are some examples of the Evil Shadow in action:

As a child, one of my clients tripped another girl on purpose during a basketball game.

Another stole money from her baby sister's piggy bank.

Another lied to her friends that she was a champion skier—despite the fact that she'd never seen snow! (That last example was me, age nine.)

Now, let's get to know the wild and untamed part of *you*.

EXERCISE
The Evil Shadow

Close your eyes.

Think back to your childhood and remember a time when you did something bad*—you stole, cheated, lied, were intentionally nasty . . .*

If you can't pull up a specific memory, think of a time when you wanted to or thought about doing something bad.

Don't worry about finding the perfect example!

Just use whatever image comes to you.

Keeping your eyes closed, push that image out in front of you . . .

See her as a separate person. She may look like you—or a distorted version of you. That's okay. Don't judge her. Simply see and feel her powerful, confident presence.

You've just met your Evil Shadow.

~

Just as with your Inferior Shadow, you might find this exercise difficult.

At first, your Evil shadow may be hazy and unclear. She may not even be human. One of my clients saw a flamboyant, green-scaled dragon with golden eyes and bright red lips! Right now, you can simply experience her as a feeling or presence. As you invite her into your life, she'll become more defined. Remember, there's a price to a pay when we're cut off from our shadows. They don't disappear—but can become warped by the influence of Madame X.

There are two common ways in which a lack of connection with your Evil Shadow may present: a tendency to be timid and insecure, or a tendency to be overbearing and self-centered.

In my twenties—the so-called golden years of my acting career—I was fiercely self-confident and narcissistic. When remembering how I behaved, I cringe. One incident in particular sticks out. I was twenty-two years old and a series regular on *Falcon Crest*. I was on some talk show, sitting next to another actress—one of the stars of a daytime soap. The host asked, "Jamie, have you ever considered doing a daytime soap?" I screwed up my face like I'd just eaten something rotten (or bit into a bar of Dial soap!) and said, "Ugh! I would *never*. They're awful!" The expression on that young woman's face is seared into my brain. Not only was she hurt, she was in utter disbelief at my rudeness. Probably the crew and half the audience felt the same way she did.

Here's another charming story from the days before I got in touch with my inner shadow selves. A TV series I'd starred in, *Lady Blue*, had just been canceled. I was sure my career was over but then I got my dream job—a recurring role with an option to become a regular on the critically acclaimed *St. Elsewhere*. I was *thrilled*. It felt like being thrown a life preserver made of brilliant writing and a stellar ensemble cast.

There was one actor who I was especially excited to be working with. I'd seen him in a movie a couple of years before and was blown away. As it turned out, my very first scene was with him. I could not *wait* to get to set that day. The master shot (where the camera sees everything from a wide angle) went great. Now it was time for individual close-ups. In close-ups, the director of photography gives you what's called an eye-line—where to look so the camera gets the best shot of you for the scene. As the star of *Lady Blue,* I was used to getting enthusiastic support when I voiced an opinion. It turned out to be a different story with *St. Elsewhere.* Way different. As the DP set up my close-up on that first day, I was eager to let everyone know this wasn't my first rodeo—and that I knew as much as (or more than) the cameraman. I thought that would make them like me. *Hey, she's contributing! And she's* right*!* (Cue applause.)

I smiled and said, loud and proud, "My eye-line should be *here*."

The actor I so admired turned to me, his eyes lit with menacing amusement. In a booming voice, he addressed the set. "Hey everyone, I have an announcement." All the work stopped as the cast and crew looked over. "The *actress* says the look should be *here*"—pointing to the spot I'd picked. It got dead quiet. Suddenly, I was Carrie at the dance, covered in pig blood; I was eight years old, sitting at the dinner table with worms of spaghetti dripping down my face.

The next day, my agent called to say he'd had a "short" conversation with the producers. "They said that *St. Elsewhere* is an ensemble show, and you need to . . . *tone it down*." He tried to downplay it, but I knew I was toast. For the rest of my contracted four episodes, I became the insecure, passive manifestation of the Evil Shadow. I showed up prepared, knew my lines cold, hit my marks, but made myself as small and unnoticeable on set as possible.

I disappeared.

The next time my agent called was to tell me that my option to be made a regular hadn't been picked up. In a short-term free fall, I was no longer a TV golden girl—it was more like I was the aluminum siding my father used to sell when his acting career was over. I was still able to get auditions but blew them because of my crippling anxiety, doubt, and fear. I didn't feel like a has-been. I felt like a never-was.

The "golden" part of the *St. Elsewhere* fiasco was that it led me to begin therapy with Dr. Stutz. He told me that I needed to learn how to drive down the middle of the road. When I was rude to the actress on that talk show, he said I'd jerked the car to the right and landed in a gully. And when my confidence was shaken on the *St. Elsewhere* set, I steered the car to the left—into oncoming traffic.

If I wanted to learn how to drive down the middle of the road, he told me that I had to embrace and love my Evil Shadow.

~

Our deepest fear is not that we are inadequate.
Our deepest fear is that we are powerful beyond measure.
—Marianne Williamson

We are all filled with longing for the wild . . . The longing lives in our skin, our cells, our bones.
—Clarissa Pinkola Estés

EXERCISE
Working with Your Evil Shadow

Close your eyes.

Bring back the image of your Evil Shadow that you discovered in the first exercise.

Keeping your eyes closed, push that image out in front of you. Make her as vivid, real, and powerful as you can. (Remember, it's okay if the image isn't human, or is just feeling.)

Lock eyes with the Shadow.

What does the Shadow think of you? Does it approve of how you're living your life?

Tell your Evil shadow that until now you've been afraid of her but your fear was misguided. Tell the Shadow that her wild vitality and power are crucial expressions of your life force.

Ask her if there is something you need to bring forward in your life—something you're avoiding because you've been afraid.

Promise to follow the Shadow's advice.

Keep your promise.

It's important to note that if your shadow tells you to do something that is injurious to you or to others, that's not the Evil Shadow, that's Madame X.

~

The difference between successful people and really successful people is that really successful people say no to almost everything.
—Warren Buffett

No is a complete sentence.
—Anne Lamott

The Power of No

The Evil Shadow has no trouble saying no—or should I say, shouting, shrieking, bellowing, "NO!"

A dear friend was having an epic birthday party. I didn't want to go. My father had died a couple of months before and I was still reeling; his passing rocked me, shifted me, terrified me, humbled me. I was in a delicate, contemplative space. I only wanted to see close friends in small groups or better yet, one-on-one. I knew the birthday girl well—and that she'd be upset if I declined her invitation.

I had come a long way from my self-centered actress days, so the issue wasn't about me having something better to do that night. As I mentioned earlier, my father suffered from Alzheimer's and I helped Mom care for him. At the time of his death, they had been married fifty-five years. Suddenly single—and with no plans of going on match.com—Reta was lost. I wanted to be there for her in every way but as the months passed, I became exhausted, both physically and psychically. As I write this, I see the absurdity of my birthday bash dilemma:

I'm fifty-seven years old and don't want to go to a seventy year old's birthday party. I asked my Evil Shadow for guidance.

Her words of wisdom?

"*Just fucking say no.*"

Like a child, I told her, "But she's gonna be *mad.* She's gonna be really *hurt.*"

My shadow looked at me challengingly. "I think she'll live."

Love or Fear

Another way to look at this party dilemma is to follow the advice of an old friend of mine. He told me that when he's unsure about a decision, he asks himself, "Am I coming from love? Or am I coming from fear?"

What was my reason to go to the party?

Because if I don't, my friend will be pissed.

Then I asked myself, What would be my reason *not* to go?

I'm still grieving. I didn't have the energy to make small talk. I was still waking up in the middle of the night in disbelief that he was gone—something I couldn't comprehend. One minute I'm in my car laughing at something I heard on a podcast; the next, I'm pulling over and crying my eyes out. I can't control that nor would I want to. It was clear that my reason go to the party would be based on fear, not love. Fear-based decisions *never* have happy endings. Madame X is fear's emissary. If fear is the driving force behind your choices, you can be sure MX is guiding your thoughts.

I told my friend that I wouldn't be coming and explained why. As expected, she was upset—*very* upset. We didn't speak for a year. From time to time, I felt guilty. I'd tell myself that

I was a terrible friend, that I should have just sucked it up and celebrated life.

Yet whenever I checked in with my shadows, they told me that my guilt was a "reverse indicator." *Reverse indicator* is a Stutzian term. We usually think we'll feel good when we do the right thing. But sometimes the only way to *know* we did the right thing is when our actions make us feel *bad*, uneasy, selfish. Sometimes doing the "right thing"—behaving in new, healthier ways—is out of our comfort zone. Feeling guilty for taking care of my needs indicated that I'd moved out my old, safe, familiar methods. When I escaped my comfort zone, I also escaped the clutching hands of Madame X.

A year after saying no to the party, I got an email from my estranged friend asking if we could have lunch. On the way to the restaurant, I was nervous. Was she going to lay into me? Was she going to say that I let her down? Was she going to tell me that all anyone talked about at the party was how awful I was? How cold, how self-obsessed? Instead, to my surprise, she apologized. "I'm sorry I made such a big deal about my birthday," she said contritely. "That was selfish. You have a perfect right to say no to anything that doesn't feel right for you. My overreaction made me realize that I set a lot of conditions in my relationships, conditions that revolve around *me*. This separation we had allowed me to see that—and become a better friend, and not just to you. So, thank you. I love you. I'd love to have you back in my life."

I was so struck by her courage and humility that I cried. We caught up on each other's lives and after the tears, laughed our asses off. Now, we have a much deeper, honest, and loving bond than ever. Ours has become one of my most treasured relationships.

Not all such encounters have happy endings. But life isn't about tidy resolutions—it's about the struggle to act from love, not fear.

EXERCISE
Love or Fear

Think of a decision that you are having trouble with and put it to the test. For example, spending money to go to a friend's "destination wedding," that you can't afford.

Reasons to go: "If I don't go, I'm afraid that my friend will resent me." Also, "Everyone I know will be there! It's going to be great." (FOMO)

Reasons not to go: I have $5,000 in credit card debt that I'm trying to pay off and it's totally stressing me out. I don't have the money for a plane ticket and a hotel (not to mention the wedding gift!). I do *have enough for a modest present—but that's it.*

It's clear that the decision coming from *love* is to send a nice gift but not go to the wedding.

Letting fear drive our decisions—putting what we perceive as other people's needs before our own—is not only detrimental to us, but to others. It's an impediment to *everyone's* spiritual growth.

Because sometimes our no becomes another person's yes.

~

There's something called Noh theater—a centuries-old, classical form of stylized Japanese dance-drama. As an homage (what can I say, I'm a stage nerd), I call the following exercise "NO Theater."

EXERCISE
NO Theater

If you want to be truly free, you must have the capacity to withstand the perceived or actual disapproval of others.

In this exercise, you will literally practice saying no.

As crazy as it may sound, I want you to look for opportunities to inconvenience and disappoint people—*the more you're rejected or disapproved of, the better.* If you feel guilty and uncomfortable, it's a reverse indicator.

It means you're doing it right.

Examples:

- The next time you're at a restaurant and something is not to your liking, send the order back. Steak over- or undercooked? *Send it back.* Not enough dressing on your salad? *Have them fix it.* If you *really* want to scare yourself, send something back just for practice. If your french fries are perfect, tell the server they're underdone. (If anyone reading this is in food service, forgive me!)

The idea is to get used to speaking up for what you want, even though it may inconvenience others. *It's okay.* You can make up for it by leaving a big tip. And never be mean about it—just politely state your wishes.

- The next time you're invited to a social event that you don't want to attend—a wedding, bar mitzvah, even coffee with an acquaintance—say no. Again, be kind. The twelve-step group Al-Anon puts it nicely: "Say what you mean, mean what you say, but don't say it mean." (My friend Nancy adds, "And only say it once!")

Make it a goal to say no at least once a week for a month (extra points for more). Note in your journal how many times you've said NO—and to whom—and how that made you feel. Add the Love or Fear exercise or the Science of Reality tool if you wish. The Love or Fear exercise will help you understand your motivations and make sure they're aligned with authentic desires. The Science of Reality tool will allow you to see the consequences, if any, of your actions.

I'm sixty-five as of this writing. At this stage of life, the ability to say no is a crucial skill. Because our lives are ruled by uncertainty, it's impossible to know how many shopping days we have left before Christmas. That's just reality. I don't write that to be morbid—I write it because it highlights that the most important currency we have is time. I can't afford to overspend on things I don't want or need; nor do I wish to be miserly, saying no to everything. As Stutz would say, drive down the middle of the road. In No Theater, that means doing what nourishes you.

Doing what you imagine might nourish *others* is a price you can't afford to pay.

~

> I found out what [Chris Rock and Dave Chappelle] were getting, and I was like, you're going to pay me the same. Otherwise, peace out.
>
> —Amy Schumer

> If you don't ask, you don't get. I had to learn to stop being "grateful" and start being assertive.
>
> —Mindy Kaling

Madame X and Money

Women have a complicated relationship to money. Those complications have deep roots in the patriarchy. It wasn't until the Equal Credit Opportunity Act of 1974 that a woman in America could get a credit card without a male cosigner. Until 1988, we couldn't even get a business loan without having a man on the application.

In my acting days, I didn't have a problem demanding my "quote," i.e. my going rate for an appearance in a film or TV show. In fact, with each successive job, it was common practice to demand *more,* in order to establish a higher number. But when I became a writer and coach, I had a hard time setting my price. I once negotiated a *lower* rate than what I'd been offered! I was doing some writing for a wealthy client who offered me $100 an hour.

"That's too much!" I said. "Pay me seventy-five."

"Okay," they said wryly. "But I won't go any lower."

Because of our longtime association and my fluency with his work, Stutz began giving me referrals. I set what I felt was a reasonable rate and quickly built a thriving practice. After a few years, I learned that a colleague was charging double my fee. I was righteously pissed. I reasoned that they'd been doing the work for just five years, against my thirty—why did they feel entitled to charge twice as much? Then I thought, wait a minute, who's the dummy here? The problem wasn't that they were overcharging. I was *undercharging.*

I took out my journal and did the Love or Fear exercise.

Why I shouldn't raise my rates:

If I charge more, people won't want to work with me. My practice will suffer and die. Also, raising my rates makes me feel greedy. If people can't afford me, what am I supposed to do—abandon them? I'm in a helping profession. How is charging more "helping"?

Why I should raise my rates:

I'm highly qualified and sincerely care about the people I work with. I'm charging way too little compared to my colleagues. But I worry about my clients' money more

> *than I do my own—I have bills to pay as well. Also, I've heard that sometimes if you charge too little, people don't think you're worth as much; so it's possible that by charging more, I might attract more clients. And I can always make exceptions by charging less when it's called for. And if someone can't afford me, I know a few great coaches who charge less and are trying to build their client list who would greatly appreciate the referrals. Maybe one of those coaches would be an even better fit.*

All of the reasons *not* to raise my rates were coming from fear.

Good Girl Syndrome

One of the hallmarks of the feminine archetype is the instinct to *connect*, with nature and with people. That characteristic is vital for the survival of humanity and the planet itself. But society has perverted those instincts into something limiting and self-negating—what financial coach Mikelann Valterra calls the "Good Girl Syndrome." Valterra has said that while negotiating, women often "fear harming the relationship itself. God forbid these wonderful people who are our clients think that we believe money is more important than people."

If we want to take up our rightful space, which includes getting paid what we deserve, we must be willing to throw off the mantle of the Good Girl. Undercharging was an overcorrection; I was trying to distance myself from my narcissistic actress days. What I *really* needed was to bring back some of that Jamie Rose-at-twenty-five Bad Girl energy.

To gather the courage to raise my rates, I needed help. So I called someone in the helping profession: my brilliant friend Barry Michels, Stutz's coauthor of *The Tools* and *Coming Alive*.

Barry said that I *had* to charge more—and not just because I was worth it. He told me that *the willingness to do so* was an essential part of my spiritual growth.

After we spoke, I paced around the room a while, then dialed 1-800-EVIL SHADOW.

I closed my eyes and made the connection. At first, the reception wasn't great . . . then slowly, the sights and sounds grew clearer. I saw a version of me in those Golden Girl Actress years—this time, though, I didn't see her as narcissistic or demanding. *This* time, she was, quite simply, fabulous. Big '80s-style hair, like a crown of curling red fire. Supremely confident, expressive, and free. She knew what she wanted and wasn't afraid to ask for everything she felt she was worth. I imagined getting on my knees and begging her for help.

"It's about time," she said.

I asked what *she* thought I should be charging.

Without hesitation, she gave me a number that instantly made me feel queasy. It's not that the quote was insane—it was still less than the colleague's fee that had so enraged me. Thankfully, I knew enough to realize that my discomfort was a reverse indicator.

I needed to go *toward* it.

I promised that wild, fierce redhead that the next time someone asked about working with me, I would quote the new rate. And kept my promise—uhm, sort of.

The very next day I got a call from someone who'd come to one of my webinars and wanted some private sessions. I steeled myself and gave the new price. The "uhm, sort of" part was that I quickly added, "But if that's too high, I can give you a friends and family rate."

Did I mention that I offered a discount before they even asked?

Afterward, I sheepishly checked in with my Evil Shadow. She shook her fiery-curled, demon goddess head. "Girl," she castigated. "*You need to get your diva back.*"

I took a deep breath, gritted my teeth, and sent out a search party. And promised myself that the next time, no matter how hard it was, I would tell a prospective client the new rate. *It didn't matter whether they hired me or not.* It wasn't about the money—it was about cutting the bonds of fear. It was about beating Madame X.

A sweet young man in his mid-twenties called to book a session. (Something about his shy demeanor reminded me of one of my beloved nephews.) I really wanted to work with him. Then came the dreaded moment: "How much do you charge?" I knew in my gut there was no way this kid could pay my rate. I imagined my shadow nudging me with a "Don't fuck this up" expression on her face. When I gave him the number, his long sigh sounded like the biggest tire in the world losing all of its air.

He muttered, "I can't afford that."

AAAAAARRGH.

My worst fears had come true. I felt selfish—cruel even. I *so* wanted to offer my famous friends and family discount! Then I remembered the promise I made to my Shadow, and my commitment to win the war against Madame X. "I'd love to work with you," I said, forcing out the words. "But I get it. How about I give you the names of some wonderful coaches who are more affordable?"

After the call, I checked in with my shadow. She smiled and said, "Good job, Diva."

Still, I felt like I'd let this kid down. I even had a weird fantasy about the colleague who'd started this whole price war. I imagined *her* Evil Shadow getting in touch with him and offering a slashed rate! So I called Barry.

"Well—*I did it.* I connected with my shadow for counsel and when I got a call from a potential client, I gave the new rate." I tried to sound proud of myself but the words were hollow. (In truth, I felt like I'd hit a deer in the road.) Barry was happy for me. Then I added, downcast, "But he couldn't afford it."

"Do you feel guilty?" he asked.

"*Very.*"

"Excellent!"

"Huh?" Everything I knew about reverse indicators went out the window.

"If it wasn't hard, Jamie, you wouldn't learn anything. I know that *you* know there's pain associated with growth—you've been telling your clients that for years. But when it comes to *ourselves*, it's a different story. The things we already know are hard to apply. We tell our clients that when we experience discomfort, that's a *good* thing—a break from the too familiar. For clients and *ourselves*, the familiar can often be a trap. That's why they call it the comfort zone. We become 'acceptable' versions of shut-ins—people who are afraid to leave the safety of their routines. To do what you did, even though it was something you feared—to take an action that you *did not want to do*—is everything. It means you did it right."

I have a client wait list now, and I've helped other coaches grow their practices. But what's most important is, my Evil Shadow helped me win another battle against Madame X.

~

Honesty without love is attack.
—Hubert Selby Jr.

Unsolicited advice is just criticism in a cardigan.
—Unknown

How to Wear a Cardigan

My client Phyllis prided herself on being blunt. The trouble was, after the smoke cleared from her truth-bombed battlefield, friends were either MIA or carried away on stretchers to be treated for the wounds she'd inflicted. Only Phyllis remained—the general who won the battle but lost the war.

"I tell it like it is!" she shouted stridently during one of our sessions. "And people *just can't take it*. They don't want to hear the truth." She looked wounded herself, which, of course, she was. "I'll tell you what I mean. Last night, I went to the opening of a friend's show at a gallery. It was horrific! The paintings weren't even derivative; it was like the exhibition of an *untalented middle-schooler*."

"Is that what you told her?"

"*Noooo*—well, not the middle school part. And not the untalented part. But I was *honest* with her, Jamie. I told her I liked the color choices—the palette, the *whatever.* I majored in art history, okay? I thought, if no one's going to tell her the truth, I guess that's going to have to be *my* job. Because she needs to hear it! I mean, it's just not fair for her to keep thinking she's friggin Frida Kahlo."

"*Does* she think she's friggin Frida Kahlo?"

"You *know* what I mean, Jamie. How can you *learn*, how can you *improve* if no one tells you the *reality*?"

"So what did she say? How did she react?"

Phyllis twisted her mouth. "I don't know . . . "

"I think that you *do*."

"Okay, she was *not* happy. She said something like 'Thanks for the feedback' then walked over to some other people—probably people who told her what a genius she was!"

"Back up a minute. Is this person a friend of yours? Or just an acquaintance?"

"She's someone I know from work."

"An acquaintance, then."

"Somewhere between friend and acquaintance, I guess. We've known each other a few months and sometimes go to lunch. Jamie, I *like* her. I just don't like her so-called art." There was something beneath her grimace—as if she knew she was being judgmental, knew how awful she sounded, but also had the awareness that she couldn't help herself. When Phyllis softened, I saw sadness there too. "I mean, she's really funny. She makes me laugh. I make *her* laugh, though not as much." She ended her comments with a defensively sardonic, "Especially not last night! Apparently."

When I asked if she thought her gallery ambush came from love or fear, she quickly answered, "Love! I was *helping* her—"

"Were you?"

My question hung in the air. Clearly, after one of her many battlefield encounters, Phyllis never dared asked herself that.

She grew up an only child in an unhappy home. Her father slept with other women and her mother tolerated it. But Mom's rage came out in other ways, often against her daughter. A skilled opera singer, she put her dreams aside when she became a wife and mother. Phyllis watched the most important woman in her life wither on the vine, tormented by a marriage that was a lie on so many levels. She wanted her mother to tell the truth about that lie (children are often wise beyond their years) but saw that she lacked the courage. When Phyllis reached adulthood, she vowed always to be transparent, to never hold back from *expressing* the truth, believing that honesty, even if savage, was essential. That blunt tool became the trait about herself that she most admired. As a result, she adopted the role of a modern-day town crier. Merciless candor was the best way to be of service to all whom she encountered. But it backfired. Friends weren't grateful, they were repelled. She hurt them and made them angry, and they vanished from her life. In the end, she felt as alone and frightened as the child who used to live in, what Phyllis called during our sessions, "The House of Lies." She became a walking example of a distorted Evil Shadow. She'd convinced herself that her brutal honesty was an asset; Madame X had trained her—so well!—to use truth like a cudgel. And to disguise that cudgel of fear as love.

Obliviously, she used it most effectively on herself.

Her face went blank when I asked if she'd really thought she was helping her artist friend by her Truth Bomb Love. She was trembling now. I touched her hand and said, "Your friend put herself out there. That's an incredibly brave, vulnerable act. What she needed was congratulations and support that she did something courageous, worthy, and right. Have you heard of Glennon Doyle?" She shook her head and stared at the floor, like a child. "Glennon wrote, 'I don't want advice, I want connection. I want empathy. I want to be *seen*, not *fixed*.' If your friend wants your opinion about her work, let her ask. And if she doesn't, don't offer it."

"I just don't want to lie," she whispered. The facade was cracking.

"You said that you liked the color palette she used, right?" Phyllis nodded. "Then how about, 'Thank you so much for inviting me. And you have an *amazing* sense of color.'"

At last, she looked up. "I guess that would have been honest."

"And loving."

Soon, she had an opportunity to put what we'd spoken of into practice. A woman she knew from church had been taking voice lessons. Her final class was a showcase at a little neighborhood theater and she invited Phyllis to come.

The woman had an attack of stage fright. Her throat closed up and she overcompensated with a sharp, shrieky tone. In session, Phyllis told me that she was "determined to accentuate the positive. But when I waited to congratulate her after the show, I panicked. *Congratulate her for* what? What the hell was I going to say?" Her anxiety was suddenly replaced by the thought of her mother, gone for several years now. She missed her terribly and reflected on all she had loved and all she lost. Tears came to her eyes as she remembered her mother's gorgeous singing voice and how wonderful it would have been if fate had allowed her to share it with the world. When Phyllis saw her friend, they embraced, and the woman melted in her arms.

"That was *so wonderful*," said Phyllis. No judgment, no critique, no course correction needed—a new kind of honesty for her, one that came from love. The hoarse, hapless singer thanked her profusely. Phyllis wistfully added, "My mom was a singer too and your performance made me think of her. I can't tell you how moved I was."

But now, it was Phyllis's voice that was breaking.

Chapter Six

Renunciation

The woman who does not require validation from anyone
is the most feared individual on the planet.
—Mohadesa Najumi

I validate my own damn existence.
—Jameela Jamil

My first acting job was in 1967. I was six years old. It was a Kool-Aid commercial starring Bugs Bunny. The setup was that Bugs had a discotheque for kids called "Kool-Aid a-Go-Go" and I was one of the dancers. After that, I was "Kid with Chicken Pox" (aka freckles) in an Armour Hot Dog commercial, followed by a tutu'd, dancing buttercup for Life cereal. What can I say? I was on a roll. My little brother did a commercial too, for Thom McAn. It wasn't that Stevie or I particularly wanted to be in showbiz—if our parents had been cobblers, we would've made shoes.

My father's career was feast or famine, so our success not only made our folks proud, but our earnings helped us survive.

My parents were thrilled that Stevie and I were so-called "working actors." Especially Dad. He loved to show off his burgeoning mini-me superstars. Whenever I booked a gig, he kvelled (Yiddish for bursting with pride), as if he was the one who'd been hired. As a devoted Daddy's girl, nothing made me happier than to please him.

My father was addicted to show business. As a young man in the 1950s, he'd been poised for stardom but with the advent of rock and roll, his style of singing—an almost operatic baritone—was out. Overnight, the vibrant Kodachrome of the man I loved more than anyone in the world became a faded black-and-white Polaroid. He never got over it, which meant I didn't either. He performed less and less as the years went by. In his forties, the singing and acting gigs—dinner theater, invitations to sing the anthem at ballgames and croon at private parties—pretty much dried up. He sold home improvement products to make ends meet. Dad always spoke of something he called P.M.A. (Positive Mental Attitude), proudly saying, "That's what makes me a great salesman." But I knew that underneath, his life had become a quiet singalong to that sad, gorgeous Chaplin song: he smiled while his heart was breaking.

When my acting career took off, he was over the moon. That was such a touching thing for me to see. He had a T-shirt printed up that said I'M VICKY GIOBERTI'S REAL FATHER—my character's name in *Falcon Crest*. In the rare times he got booked to do his club act, I became a big part of the onstage patter. Dad would announce my presence to the audience as if to let them know how crazy lucky they'd gotten to breathe the same air as his famous daughter. One night, he held up a giant poster of me as Lady Blue in full cop regalia, holding a .357 Magnum. In an imaginary duet with the cardboard Lady, he sang, "Once in Love with Amy," but changed the name to Jamie (of course he did). He commanded everyone to sing along. Awkward? *Very.* I acted the good sport. Anything to make him happy.

My success wasn't only for me, it was for *us*.

From nineteen to twenty-six, my career was in a steady climb. I got lucky; unlike my parents, I'd never had to pay my dues, as the saying goes. (Unless you counted "Kool-Aid A-Go-Go" and "Kid with Chicken Pox.") The flatlining *St. Elsewhere* experience was my first adult-sized rejection. Trouble was, I had no experience in bouncing back. Like a boxer who goes down for the count after one punch, my jaw was made of glass. Because my entire identity was based on my acting career, when it went into free fall, the feeling of letting Dad down made the descent even worse.

I remember being with him at breakfast at Patys, one of our favorite family haunts. The classic '60s coffeeshop (still there, unchanged) was where I often ran into actors I'd worked with in TV. Many of them went on to become big stars. They liked the hominess of the place and still gathered there on the down-low; no one bothered them. By then, my father hadn't had a paid acting or singing job in years. He had just auditioned to be a regular performer on a cruise line—his cohorts called it "the cruise circuit"—but got passed over. He was visibly depressed and we ate in silence.

Then he said, "I'm nothing."

My chest caved in when I heard that. "You're *not* nothing, Dad, you're my father. I love you."

He shook his head as if he hadn't heard. "My style of singing is over," he said. "I'm over."

"Then, I'm nothing too."

"No, you are *not*," he shouted.

"But I'm not working *either*—"

With great tenderness, he took my hand and said, "You're a star."

Sometimes I felt like I was carrying my father on my back. I loved him and wanted to rescue him from Showbiz Hell. And it wasn't just Dad that needed rescuing; I wanted to save us *both* from oblivion. It was complicated. To get us out of the quicksand, I began auditioning with a vengeance. But when you come from a place of need and desperation, the story doesn't end well.

At that time, I hadn't depleted my savings (yet), so it wasn't about money. It was about my essential worth as a human being. I was no longer showing up in front of casting directors to express my artistry or interpretation of the material—I was there to convince them to fucking hire me. *That* was the fix I needed. Getting hired meant I was *something*, not "nothing." Like animals smelling fear, the casting people, producers and directors could *feel* it, sense it. Auditions became a nightmare of first dates. Instead of saying, "I'm Jamie—so nice to meet you," I led with, "I'm Jamie—LOVE ME! WANT ME! HIRE ME! FUCKING VALIDATE ME!" Thinking of that time now, I laugh. I remember the Albert Brooks line from *Broadcast News*: "Wouldn't this be a great world if insecurity and desperation made us more attractive? If 'needy' was a turn-on?"

When you're madly chasing your inauthentic self, you begin to notice that you can't even smile while your heart is breaking. I was a basket case. I showed up at auditions with sweaty palms and shaky legs; I forgot my lines or got distracted if it seemed the people in the room weren't interested. Aaron Spelling often hired me for his shows. When he brought me in for the lead in a new pilot, I sat in a chair across from him and the production staff. During my read, I noticed that one of the writers was zoning out. I put down my script, stared him down, and said, "Can you please pay attention?"

The room went quiet.

Heads turned to Aaron to see what he would do. After a long, uncomfortable moment, he calmly said, "You're absolutely right. Everyone! All eyes on Jamie."

I started the scene again. I was stiff and self-conscious and miserable. It was like the sequel to the *St. Elsewhere* fiasco. I didn't get the job and Aaron never called me in again. When I left, everyone must have thought they dodged a bullet—a bullet I had aimed at myself.

The more I blew my auditions, the more I blew my auditions. After each one, I obsessively called my agent, asking, "Did you hear anything?" But actors always know when they don't get the job. The audition may have gone beautifully, but you end up not getting cast because of your look, your chemistry, your whatever. If you got the booking, the call usually comes to your agent the same day. I don't know how it works now but that's the way it was. If you didn't hear *that day or the next*, it was over. Still, I blew up my agent's phone for a week. *What part of dead silence didn't I understand?* When I was finally forced to accept reality, I would get deeply depressed. Like my father that time at Patys, I felt like I was nothing. My life was over, all that. And in a way it was, because the only time I felt alive was when I was working. Everything but jobs and auditions was useless bullshit. The old expression says that life isn't a dress rehearsal, but they got it wrong. Life is an audition that doesn't end with a job. I was a fricking mess.

That's when a friend from acting class told me about a shrink named Phil Stutz.

I had the brilliant idea that he'd teach me how to overcome my nerves so I could start getting booked again. But at our very first session, he stared me down and said, "Your problem is that you're addicted to validation—not only that, you want it from show business! That's like a sheep going to the wolf for validation." He leaned forward. In a low, almost scary tone, he said, "Listen to me very carefully. If you don't change *and* you become successful again, you're fucked. You'll be like all the other Hollywood assholes who end up in my office five times a week. There's only one way you can save yourself. But expect to feel like shit for the next eight months."

I began to think I'd picked the wrong shrink. Yet, something about his passion, his irreverence, his *clarity* made me listen.

"For now," he said, "I don't *want* you to get an acting job. If you feed your addiction, you won't learn anything—you'll just be strung out, looking for the next fix. Here's the thing: If you can learn to be happy while experiencing constant rejection, you'll be free."

That's when he taught me Renunciation.

THE TOOL
Renunciation
(P.S.)

There's an acronym for this tool: SUVT—Support, Understanding, Validation, and Truth.

You practice renunciation when you go into a situation—a job interview, a first date, a conversation with your boss—where you want a specific outcome. The idea is to accept the possibility of not getting what you want. You "go in" not expecting the support of that other person. You don't expect them to understand or validate you, you don't even expect them to share your reality. But *renunciation* is far stronger than simple acceptance. Not only do you accept that you may not get any validation from outside yourself, you renounce even the *hope* of getting what you want. You become want-less. Paradoxically, the SUVT mindset boosts your chances of getting what you want. Because, in this state of renunciation, you become self-validating—free from the bonds of approval-seeking that tie you to the material world.

This makes you unstoppable.

Back then, Stutz didn't call his techniques the Tools. He called them the Protocol. My audition protocol was to be one hundred percent prepared—learn the scenes cold, dress appropriately for the character, and arrive on time (which meant ten minutes early). He also gave me some visualization techniques to do before and during auditions, which I'll explain later in this chapter.

In my case, he said that what I did after the audition—what he called the *afterburn*—was especially important. I needed a plan: to have coffee with a friend, visit a museum, or get my car washed . . . it didn't matter what the plan was, just that I had one. I was also instructed not to call my agent, under any circumstances!

"Your job now," he said, "isn't to get the job. Your job is to do the Protocol—to *pride* yourself on doing the Protocol. The Protocol is the only success you care about because it's the only thing you have control over. This your new definition of success."

Instinctively, I knew that if I didn't follow Stutz's instructions I was doomed to enter a misery loop. It was tremendously difficult at first but it didn't take long for me to begin having fun at my auditions. What a concept! The auditions became a kind of game, a quiet dare. "What are you gonna do, reject me? Ha! I *thrive* on rejection. I'm a rejection eater!" I was a boxer who was training to exchange a glass jaw for one of iron. Every time they knocked me down, I stood up as fast as I could. "Go ahead. Hit me again!"

I'd won even before stepping into the ring.

As it turned out, instead of feeling like shit for the eight months, I only felt like shit for eight weeks. (And I mean real shit—not fun.) Maybe the eight-month proclamation was a genius Stutzian maneuver that was meant to toughen me up and lower my expectations. But I followed the Protocol. I smiled while my heart was breaking and when it stopped breaking, the smile got bigger. Life got bigger too. Life began to feel more real than auditions.

Imagine that.

~

I'd like to tell you that through all this work on myself, I evolved into a perfect, light-filled being. As it turned out, I had to learn the same lessons over and over again. In 2010, mapping the outline of my first book, *Shut Up and Dance!*, I heard about an agent who was looking for self-help books written by women. My mantra became, "All I want is to finish this proposal so I can send it to her." I did and she took me on. Then my mantra became, "All I want is to sell this book." The day the little penguin-stamped contract arrived, I cried. It meant more to me than any acting role I'd ever had.

What I couldn't see was how closely the experience mirrored what happened to me as an actor; the same kind of lightning success without paying dues. I was too happy—or too unwise or too taken with myself—to see the parallel, and more ominously, the potential pitfalls. *Love me! Need me! Want me! Read me!* The new mantra became, "All I want is for my book to become a bestseller."

It didn't.

I crawled back to the strung-out world I'd known so well. I obsessed over my rank on Amazon, logging in every fifteen minutes to check the numbers like a lab rat hitting a food pellet lever. As the weeks went by, I began to think I was hitting the wrong lever, because . . . where were the pellets? *Who the eff is stealing my pellets!*

One day, defeated and exhausted, I stopped checking. In a familiar Patys state of mind, I stared into space and intoned my old-new mantra:

I am nothing.

Now, here's a little fish story for you.

Growing up, my favorite book was *Grimm's Fairy Tales.* A story called "The Fisherman and His Wife" always haunted me. Once upon a time, a poor fisherman and his wife lived in a filthy hovel by the sea. One day, the fisherman caught a large flounder—but this was no ordinary creature of the sea. It stood on its tail and said, "I am not a real fish but an enchanted prince. Throw me back into the sea and let me live! Besides, there's no use cooking me because I will taste awful."

"Of course I'll throw you back!" said the fisherman, in awe and delight.

When he came home, he told his wife of his wondrous experience with the magic fish.

"You fool!" she admonished. "An enchanted prince? You should have asked him to grant you a wish! Go back, go back! And ask the flounder for a better house."

So he did, and the grateful flounder granted his wish. It wasn't enough for the fisherman's wife. Again and again, she sent him back for upgrades: a charming cottage, a grand stone manor, a glittering palace crowned with towers. But her hunger wasn't satisfied. She asked to be made Queen, seated on a golden throne. Then, Empress, ruling all the lands. Then,

Pope, worshipped by commoners and kings. Finally she said, "I shall command the sun and the moon and bend the heavens to my will, and be lord of the universe! My wish is to become God."

With his head hung low, the fisherman returned to the flounder with his final wish. The flounder listened, sighed, then sent him home—back to the palace, which had once again become a hovel.

Why, as a child, would that fable so intoxicate me? Now, as an adult, I see it as a cautionary tale that foretold my professional fall(s) from grace and even my bankruptcy.

Stutz talks about two paradigms of being in the world. He calls them Universe One and Universe Two. If you live in Universe One, your concern is winning or losing. Your worth and value are defined numerically—how much money you have, your Amazon rank, your zip code, your weight, your fitness tracker score, your muscle to fat ratio, number of children, and age.

Madame X rules Universe One.

Universe Two is ruled by the Divine Feminine. She doesn't bother with numbers, looks, or achievements. She only cares about creativity and connection. In Universe Two, value is based on what you're giving, not what you're getting back.

I'd like to share with you a traumatic experience that could have brought down the house of powerful awareness I was so carefully building through my long years of work with the Tools. Earlier, I mentioned that I had to learn the same lessons, over and over. That's part of the human experience—falling down. But the work we do is not about avoiding the tumble, it's about getting up. As quickly as we can.

Stutz calls it the Turnaround.

~

Fall seven times, stand up eight.
—Japanese proverb

Success is stumbling from failure to failure
with no loss of enthusiasm.
—Winston Churchill

The Saturday Night Massacre

Phil and I were at a well-known retreat center in northern California doing a weekend seminar. Several events were happening at the same time and the center asked if the leaders wanted to offer a free, one-hour sample seminar on Saturday night while classes and workshops were on break.

It was the first time I was officially teaching with Stutz.

I was feeling excited and confident. Stutz was exhausted from our sessions and suggested that I do the "sample" by myself, thinking it would be good for me to stake my claim as an independent teacher of his work. I eagerly agreed. I was ready—I'd been sober from drugs and alcohol for more than thirty-five years and done hundreds of speaking engagements for that community. For most of my life, I'd been a professional actor and would draw on that experience as well. My ability to read the room, my ease on stage, and foundational experience with improv would serve me well.

When I share the story of my sobriety in front of large and small groups, I never have a set speech. In other words, I'm not reading from a script. I talk about what my life was like before the drinking starting, how and why I stopped, and what my life has been like since. I always do a spiritual preparation, handed down to me from a sober friend, as a kind of meditation:

Keep me Humble, Keep Me Honest,
Show Me How to be of Service

It made sense that the trusty template would work just fine: What my life was like before finding Stutz and the Tools, what brought me to the work, and how the work changed my life.

As the audience streamed in, I felt the same nervous excitement I'd had on opening nights or the first day of a film shoot—a little scared, but exhilarated. I mingled with the crowd and introduced myself, thanking them for showing up (which soothed my nerves as well). I especially hit it off with three young women. I was *feeling* it—my own little group of cheer-leaders . . . *fun.* Soon there were more than a hundred people in the room, what my showbiz parents called SRO (Standing Room Only). I felt alive and electric, bigger than life. Words blinked in my head like a neon marquee: *I'm going to kill.* My eyes landed on Stutz, my beloved mentor. He was sitting in the front row, ready to watch his protege take the wheel. Doing the sample talk allowed Stutz to have a much-needed break and that made me happy.

All day long, I'd done the Protocol meditation: *Keep me humble, keep me honest, show me how to be of service.* I connected with my shadows, asking them to stay with me throughout the talk. For good measure—after all, this *was* my solo Tools teaching debut—I added some tried and true Stutzian tools called Dusting and Radiation.

Radiation is the first Tool that Stutz ever taught me (back in the '80s, there were only a handful), and it is one of the Tools I use the most to this day.

THE TOOL
Radiation
(P.S.)

Close your eyes.

Imagine the atmosphere of the room you're in is filled with a feeling of love, peace, and goodwill. If you need help conjuring this feeling, imagine walking through a redwood forest or watching a beautiful sunset or kissing a newborn infant's soft skin. Whatever evokes a feeling of gentle bliss.

Imagine that the room you are in is filled with that blissful feeling.

Now, breathe in this sense of peace and love, imagining it as a golden light. Feel this golden light enter your heart. As you breathe, the light begins to expand . . . so much so that it spills out from your heart and saturates the room you're in, bathing everything in warm, golden light.

Again, the light enters your heart, expands, and spills back out. Your heart is like a fountain of light. Bubbling over, flooding the room with golden radiance.

Keep the cycle going. Bring the light back into your heart—feel it expand and spill out again.

Now, open your eyes but keep doing the Tool . . .

I love this Tool because it transports me to a calm, outflowing state. And I can do it anywhere—with eyes open. The Radiation Tool is especially effective when used in combination with another early Tool called Dusting. Dusting helps you let go of the need for external validation. When done alongside the Radiation Tool, it potentiates self-expression. Dusting is a very simple tool that is useful for situations where you might be inclined to seek the approval of others—a job interview, public speaking, even a holiday dinner with your family. (For those readers who tensed up at the last example, do these Tools immediately!)

THE TOOL
Dusting
(P.S.)

Imagine your "audience"—a coworker, friend, a family member. You're in a room with them. The room is coated in a thick layer of dust, like an empty attic that no one's entered in years.

Your "audience" is also covered with dust.

The key to the visualization is that the dust is flat, dull, non-emanating. It emits no light. When Dusting, strive to have the feeling that nothing will come your way from your "audience" or situation.

That's Dusting—it's that simple.

Dusting is a wonderful Tool to use along with Radiation. When you do them together, *you* are the source of light. You're in a state of outflow, expecting nothing to return to you. This Tool creates a paradox—the more you dust the people around you and give up hope of getting their validation, the more enlightened you'll be in your interactions.

~

Back to the Massacre!

Onstage at the retreat center, I felt relaxed and connected. All my shadows were present and accounted for. I had dusted—and was radiating like a MF. I smiled at my trio of cheerleaders, who were beaming at me with adorable, diehard enthusiasm.

Relaxed and self-assured, I began my talk.

As a preamble, I recounted my dazzling career as an actress—and how I turned in desperation to Dr. Phil Stutz when my celebrity went south. The crowd was with me, laughing in all the right places and nodding their heads in affirmation. *I was in the zone.* So on I went. I filled in more details about my life, you know, the spiel about being a kid TV actor, running my own acting studio, then teaching theater at the university level . . . as I meandered, the mood of the audience seemed to curdle. Amid the restless stirring and whispers, I glanced at Stutz—he looked confused. *Oh shit.* The cheerleaders were still beaming but their frozen smiles looked ready to crack. By then, it didn't take an actor's sixth sense to read the room: a dark gray cloud of WTF hung from the ceiling, blotting out the sun of their enthused expectations.

I was only fifteen minutes into an hour-long talk when, in a seizure of clarity, I realized that I was in deep trouble. These people were here to learn about the teachings of Dr. Stutz. Instead, I was pitching the Jamie Rose biopic.

And had forty-five minutes to go.

Without warning, I had entered a nightmare—I was paralyzed but my mouth kept talking, even as people began to leave. Still, my show-must-go-on DNA kicked in. I began teaching a simple Tool called Active Love but was so frazzled, I taught it wrong. Someone in the audience kindly corrected me. When I looked over at Phil, he was bug-eyed, like he couldn't believe what he was seeing. For me, it was hellishly immersive; I got thrown back to the torment of blowing an audition or forgetting my lines in the middle of a play. Herds of attendees were heading for the exits now, without even bothering to be sneaky about it—my cheerleaders were gone, leaving only shredded pompoms behind. And I'm still flailing. A walking, talking, anti-advertisement for the Tools.

By the time I finished (at last!), the only ones left were our Tools group. Like good soldiers, they weakly shouted "Great job!" before going MIA. Stutz was the last to come over. He hugged me and said, "Let's talk tomorrow." A master of dark humor, he didn't even have the heart to make a joke! *That's* how bad it went. I'd let both of us down. I felt like shit and wanted to fly home.

I'd fallen hard and the question that remained was, how fast would I get up?

How long would it take to do the Stutzian Turnaround?

Afterburn

When I crawled back to my room, the first thing I did was connect with my Shadows.

I reassured the little girl with the braces and neckgear that she was perfect, safe, and loved. I thanked the ballsy, spirited woman (my Evil Shadow) with the mane of fiery curls for giving me the courage to show up—and for staying with me even when the ship was going down and the cheerleaders, women, and children were helping each other into lifeboats.

I reminded myself that this was the first time I'd ever taught Stutz's work on my own. It was wishful thinking to believe I could play that role perfectly. It would have been nice if it hadn't gone *horribly,* but you can't rule the world, let alone control it. I busily reviewed what had gone wrong, and why. I'd worked the Protocol, hadn't I? I connected with my shadows and embraced my mantra . . . right? Then it hit me, like the floor hits a face plant:

I hadn't rehearsed the content of the Tools that I planned to discuss.

In that moment, I realized that Stutz's work is spiritual in nature; *that* was why I'd conflated it with the type of talks I gave to folks who were in recovery. And because I'd been doing Stutz's practice for decades, I fell into the trap of believing myself to be an *expert*—so much for the "keep me humble" part of my meditation. We often spend a lot of time beating ourselves up after we make a mistake. We indulge in obsessive rumination and endlessly replay the event. We victimize ourselves over and over, and the self-flagellation can extend for years. We buy a cottage on Pain Lane and move in.

Madame X lives on that cul-de-sac too, but her cottage is a marble mansion. It's on a dead-end for a reason—living there will kill you.

~

Images affect us on a much deeper level than words. That's why so many athletes use visualization to enhance their performance; effective visualization not only increases self-confidence but fires neural impulses to muscles, priming them for performance. When you mindlessly relive your mistakes, you're using this powerful technique *against* yourself.

To combat this, Stutz created a Tool called the Principle of Correction.

THE TOOL
The Principle of Correction
(P.S.)

Close your eyes and return in your imagination to the moment when you behaved in a way that you regret.

Once you've identified the exact moment you made your error, ask yourself what you wish you would have done instead.

Now, rewrite the narrative. Like reshooting a scene in a film, see yourself behaving in the way you would have wanted. Make the imagery as vivid and real as you can, as if this new way of reacting is what actually happened.

~

Like a Horror Channel movie marathon, Madame X wanted me to indefinitely screen the film of the Saturday Night Massacre. Instead, I shot a new version. Relentlessly working the Principle of Correction, I saw myself teaching the seminar again—but this time, shaped by the information revealed to me in the Afterburn. As a result, I felt empowered and couldn't wait to teach that seminar again. I understood that the Massacre was pivotal. It was essential to my growth, in the same way that so many of my “failures” and disappointments had been in the past.

The bottom-line? Comfort never built a warrior.

Stutz says that there are only three certainties in life: uncertainty, a degree of pain, and ceaseless effort. Money, accomplishment, and acquisition are the spoils of Universe One—but none of those things help us deal with an uncertain future. One of the most important tools is the Turnaround—the ability to get back on our feet when we’re knocked down, and rise up faster each time. When the Turnaround becomes second nature, we enter the realm of Universe Two—a world of creation, fulfillment, and true confidence.

Chapter Seven

Action

We can't control results; all we can do is act,
and action itself creates forward motion.
—Phil Stutz

Nothing happens until something moves.
—Albert Einstein

I've had more than a few clients who have been faced with financial difficulties, loss of employment, business failures, bad investments, bankruptcy. They come to our sessions in despair. Madame X tells them their lives are over. Even though there's no longer a "debtors' prison," the fearsome picture she paints makes them feel locked in a steel cage. They are paralyzed—just where X wants to them to be. But there is a way out: through *action.*

The 4 Laws of Action

Stutz has a concept he calls The 4 Laws of Action: Speed, Density, Pre-Win, and Death Cookie.

Speed

Speed is a force. When you know what action you need to take, the more time that elapses before you take that action, the weaker you get.

Density

Take as many actions as possible. The more the better.

Pre-Win

The moment you take the action, you're a success, no matter the result of that action. For example, if you need to make an important phone call to a person who intimidates you, the moment you dial the number, you've won.

Death Cookie

All actions contain a bit of sacrifice. "Death cookie" means you identify the action that is the hardest and do that *first.*

Isaac Newton wrote that "a body in motion tends to stay in motion." If you're *stuck*, the only way out is to *move*—and get into action. Then, very often, miracles happen.

I know this first hand.

The Gift of Desperation

Aside from working part-time during high school (babysitting, retail clerking, and "canvassing" neighborhoods for the home improvement company Dad worked for), I'd only had one job since I was six years old: Acting. True, I took a break during *Jamie Rose: the Braces-and-Neckgear Years*. But then the whole thespian thing started up again at nineteen. A year later, I dropped out of college because I got cast in *Falcon Crest*. With the help of serious TV money, I bought a house when I was twenty-three—then sold it, going in on a new place when I met my first husband, who bought me out of my share when we got divorced. With *that* money, I got a condo in Santa Monica. I was free, thirty, and in love with being newly single. Top of the world, right? That's what I thought.

I was never so wrong in my life.

Growing up, my folks lived from job to job, paycheck to paycheck. Without financial security, raising kids is brutal. They maxed their credit cards and ran up so much debt that they were forced to declare bankruptcy. Twice. An indelible memory is of Mom sitting at the kitchen table, solemnly cutting up the Diners Club and Sears cards with a garden shear–size pair of scissors. I still wince when I remember the day that she told me and my brother—I was six and Stevie was four—to sign over the $25 savings bonds Grandma Sally gave us on our birthdays because they couldn't make the rent. We had no idea what bonds were but it was clear that something was rotten in the City of Angels. The mood was solemn, shot through with her shame.

My brother, who eventually became a partner at the law firm of a close associate of Warren Buffett, was determined *never* to go through what our folks did. Stevie's light reading—at nine years old, and I mean it—was "How to Make a Million in Real Estate." My own scholarly research focused on *Seventeen* and *Tiger Beat*. When I got *Falcon Crest*, I had zero idea what to do with the weekly checks, so I hired a business manager. The money went directly to Ray, who paid all my bills. I had a checking account for day-to-day spending and that's it. Looking back, it was like hiring a dad to give me an allowance.

I *wish* I could tell you Ray stole all my money but those were the golden years when actors getting ripped off by business managers wasn't yet the norm. If Ray had gone AWOL to the Amalfi Coast or I'd lost my nest egg at Hollywood Park, that would have been a better story. If I blew everything on coke and rehabs, well yeah, another cliché, but a colorful one. (Somewhat.) But I got sober at twenty-two—and stayed that way as I heisted my *own* bank accounts.

My problem? Compulsive shopping.

Shopping was my *only* interest other than acting. Malls were my bars. As a drinker, I never had a blackout but shopping was another story. I'd go into a mall and stumble out five hours later, a glassy-eyed beast of burden weighed down by bags of new clothes. It was never enough. Instead of "the fisherman's wife," I was the brand name's wife; there was always something newer, hipper, and more gorgeous that I coveted and needed to have. *Now!* When Carrie Fisher famously said "Instant gratification takes too long," whoa, did I relate. Salespersons became my close, personal friends in the same way that cokeheads think of their dealers and drinkers their bartenders. It wasn't even about *wearing* the clothes, it was about the thrill of the purchase. A costumer from a film came to my house once to see if there was anything we could use from my wardrobe. "Why do all your clothes still have tags on them?" she asked.

Thinking of it now, she probably thought I was a shoplifter.

A few hours after a binge, I'd be flooded with regret mixed with a serotonin dip—not a good combo. The next day, I would return most of what I bought. (Diagnosis: shopping bulimia.) Bloomingdale's even sent me a letter, flagging the frequency of my returns and asking if I had a problem with the quality of their products. Clearly, it was a polite way of saying, "Stop it! Or *seek help.*" It felt like Mom and Dad caught me smoking pot.

I was seeing Stutz during that time. When I told him about my compulsion, he asked, "How much money do you have in your checking account right now?"

"I don't know. Enough I guess?"

Stutz got that trademark, scary look of fatal seriousness. "That's dangerous," he said. "You need to know at all times how much money you have in your accounts. To the dime."

The condo I bought in Santa Monica after the divorce was a first-floor unit sandwiched between two hulky apartment buildings. The place had very little natural light—my "views" were a trash-strewn alley and a geriatric neighbor's living room. That old man with the hacking cough listened to opera round the clock. I started to lose it; what I thought would be my sanctuary became a waiting room in hell. But I tried to make my peace, because, well . . . I was newly single and blocks from the ocean! (And close to a half-dozen retail meccas.) Not long after escrow closed, the LA real estate market crashed. Since I wasn't planning on selling anytime soon, I wasn't rattled; I could hold out until the market recovered, as it always does. I wasn't making *Falcon Crest* money anymore but at least I was still working. The important thing was that I could still support my habit:

Charles Jourdain heels, designer bags, Betsey Johnson dresses, and the occasional jewelry splurge.

Life was good.

Because of Stutz, auditioning itself was no longer a torment and I was often in the running for big roles. But there was a little problem: my rival always got the job. As I slid (shopped?) into my mid-thirties, my career path eerily began to resemble Dad's. The worse I felt, the more I spent. I got into heavy credit card debt. Stutz gave me the obvious advice—*stop shopping*—but I couldn't. It's like that old joke, "How many psychiatrists does it take to change a light bulb? One—but the light bulb has to want to change." Or, as I say about practicing alcoholics, "You can lead a horse to water but you can't make them not drink." My business manager tried giving me course corrections as well. Whenever I called Ray and asked him to put more money in my personal checking account, he'd say, "Jamie, you're spending more than you're making." It didn't matter what Ray or Stutz or *anyone* told me.

I shopped while my career burned.

When I was young, newly sober, and *Falcon Crest* was a hit, I remember having dinner at a fancy restaurant in LA. I recognized the guy pouring our water. "Hey," I said. "Aren't you Michael Gray? From *Shazam*?" *Shazam* was a Saturday-morning live-action show for kids. Gray had been a cover boy on teenybopper fanzines when I was a young; a picture of him was taped to my bedroom wall. "Yeah," he said, face flushed. He couldn't even look at me. (Someone else came back for water refills.) The encounter became an anecdote—the whole thing was so outlandish that I had no idea it was actually an omen.

A whisper from the Ghost of Showbiz Yet to Come . . .

When I finally put my condo on the market, months went by without an offer. Buyers were turned off by the darkness and claustrophobic views. I kept lowering the price until it was $100,000 less than what I originally paid. Still, nothing. I was "underwater"—the horribly graphic, technical term for when you owe the bank more than what the place is worth. It was 1994 and I was barely working. Because of my pathological spending, I accrued over $20,000 in credit card debt. I could no longer afford my weekly visits with Stutz, let alone my favorite form of self-medication—trips to the mall for compulsive shopping. I got a roommate but was still draining my savings to make my mortgage payments. The financial walls were closing in.

I was terrified.

I never even finished college. Acting was my only skill. *What the fuck was I going to do?* Madame X had me in her grip. The worst thing was, I couldn't sleep. Sleep had always been a problem, even when my life and career were fantastic. The insomnia became exacerbated by my refusal to take sleeping pills because of my sobriety. I laid awake at night riddled with anxiety, playing a nonstop loop of nightmarish scenarios in my head. Would I end up on the street? Or living in my car (before it was repossessed)? I could already see one of those embarrassing "Where are they now" articles in the tabloids.

I wanted out. I was more than a decade sober and knew that drinking would only make my problems worse. I'd be in the same situation but drunk on top of it—a fate worse than death. I thought about killing myself but was too scared to act on it. If I was afraid of death, I was more afraid of life. Frozen: a failed actor in the headlights of uncertainty and nothingness, for which there seemed no remedy. I fell back on the lessons of my early recovery days and became willing to stay alive one day at a time. Sometimes it was one hour, sometimes it was one minute.

Then came the intervention: the 1994 LA earthquake hit. As it happened, my condo committed suicide *for* me. The walls cracked open and the insulation spilled out in ragged clumps. The bathtub shifted a foot off the drain. FEMA declared it "yellow listed"—I wouldn't be able to move back until making major repairs. The deductible for my earthquake coverage was $30,000 and I had less than $4,000 in the bank. The bank foreclosed. Like my parents before me, I declared bankruptcy and found a cheap apartment in West Hollywood. The moment I sat down in the new place, in a crummy easy chair donated by a friend, the phone rang—it was Ray, my long-suffering business manager.

"Jamie?"

"Hi Ray! Guess where *I* am? My new place. It's sweet," I lied. "I'm going to make it work!"

He got real quiet, before saying, "I'm sorry, Jamie. I just can't help you anymore."

Oh my God, I thought. *Ray has a terminal illness!*

"What do you mean? Are you okay?"

"Jamie," he stammered. "I just can't be your business manager anymore. And even if I felt comfortable with that, there's no business to *manage*. I wish you the best. I loved my time working with you—you're like family. That's what makes this so hard."

There was only one thing to do: panic.

I knew how to write a check—thank you, Bloomies!—but balancing the books was way above my pay grade. (Everything's above your pay grade when you have no income.) So, I got by with a little help from my friends. They schooled me in basic bookkeeping and told me to keep a record of everything I spent. I know it sounds obvious but that's the way it was. My clients have reinforced the notion that many of us often have gaping holes in what are generally assumed to be the common-sense strategies of navigating life.

It wasn't until my mid-thirties that I finally learned a basic lesson: if you make a dollar, don't spend a dollar and a half unless you want to go into debt! Over the next several months, I got a few little acting jobs that along with occasional residual checks kept my head above water. In that awful year, I came perilously close to having nothing in my bank account. Mom and Dad stepped in. Both were still working hard to make ends meet but found a way to give me $500 a month. I felt like shit—*so* ashamed. The celebrity who bought a house in the Hollywood Hills at twenty-three was now a has-been, mooching off her aging, struggling parents. I was right where Madame X wanted me. I could see her burning the midnight oil in hell, busily pecking out the *Where are they now* tabloid copy on a melting, fiendish typewriter.

I wasn't special anymore. The days of easy money were done; it was fun and free drinks while it lasted but the pity party was over. As they say in twelve-step groups, I needed to become "fully self-supporting by my own contributions." Time to get a job.

The trouble was, I had no skills. I'd played a doctor on TV—a lawyer, a real estate agent, a cop, and a sex worker—but in real life, I only knew how to memorize lines and hit my mark. I promised myself that I'd say yes to whatever job came along. Almost immediately, an acquaintance offered me work at their boutique for $10 an hour. The small, high-end shop was in Malibu, next door to a crazy-expensive restaurant called Nobu (its early days in LA), a favorite haunt of Hollywood A-listers. The Ghost of Showbiz Yet To Come came back to haunt me, right on time. At the boutique's door, I found myself greeting actors I had worked with, and producers and writers in whose shows I'd starred. They excitedly asked, "Is this your store?" I could tell they were conjuring the *interesting* idea that my TV money had given me the chance to pivot to a new chapter in life. "Nope," I'd reply. "Just working here."

Awkward.

One day, a woman came into the shop and eyed me curiously as she browsed. After a bit of circling, she approached. "Weren't you on *Falcon Crest*?"

"I was!" I said, "Will that be cash, check, or card?"

Shazam!

The store was aptly named the Crush Boutique. *Ego* crush for me.

A close friend stopped by to stage an intervention. "Jamie," she said. "There's a difference between humility and humiliation. You can do better than ten dollars an hour—you probably have more skills than you realize. *Do some research.*"

I'd always been a yoga fanatic. There was a beautiful yoga studio near my apartment and it turned out they were looking for instructors. I discovered an unexplored passion for teaching and soon led packed classes three times a week. At the same time, my friend Rhonda, a film buyer, hired me to do script coverage—writing up detailed synopses of books and screenplays. Decades of work as an actor and a lifetime of avid reading made me a natural.

Doors were opening. That's when I met my future ex-husband, Kip. We fell in love and in a few months decided to move in together. Kip was a working actor who, unlike my father, had survived the pitfalls of the business. He knew how to carefully save his money. He bought a house for us to live in. We weren't yet married but because I was having a tough time, he graciously paid for basic living expenses.

Even with his help, I was still broke.

Rhonda left her job and the script coverage gig went away. The house with Kip was too far from where I taught yoga, so I reached out to local studios in Malibu. But the town was crawling with instructors—a nonstarter. My twelve-year-old car broke down and needed to be replaced. Because I wasn't contributing, I was reluctant to ask Kip for help. When my parents gave me the down payment for new wheels, all those old, bad feelings came back. Just when things were looking up, there I was again: a money-sucking barnacle on the hull of my family and new partner. I was also reluctant to call Stutz with an update because I couldn't afford to pay for his time. (Anyway, there was no more room on the hull.) Luckily, I'd seen him so often during my flush years that he lived in my head. I knew what he'd say—*Keep going—stay in forward motion.*

So . . . skills! An obvious one was becoming an acting coach but I had always been resistant to that idea because I'd bought into the old saw, "Those who can't do, teach." Teaching meant I had failed, giving up on my chosen profession. But I had the gift of desperation—and was willing to do whatever I took. It was time to obey the 4 Laws of Action.

I immediately got to work (*Speed*). First, I made a list of everyone I knew who taught acting (*Density*) then called each person (*Pre-Win*). One of them told me about a small theater in the Valley that rented space during the day at a cheap rate, inexpensive enough that I could make it work with just three paying students. I booked an appointment to check it out (*Pre-Win*). On the way to meet the theater owner, I ran into Nancy Allen at Starbucks. Nancy was an old friend who'd had a much bigger career than mine, starring in movies like *RoboCop, Dressed to Kill,* and *Blow Out.* She transitioned from acting to become executive director of an iconic LA nonprofit cancer support center called WeSpark. At WeSpark, clients are offered everything from Reiki to tai chi to cooking classes, all at no charge. When I told her about my Just Say Yes to teaching plan she said, "I'd love you to do that for our clients." When she made the offer, even though it was gratis, I tapped into a primal enthusiasm that matched the pure passion I used to have for acting itself.

In teaching nonactors at WeSpark—all in different stages of their illness and recovery—it was important the classes be fun and easy. I didn't want there to be text memorization because going through chemo and facing uncertainty was stressful enough. My class needed to be a safe place where the clients could take a break from the trauma of their journey. I realized that we should be playing theater games—but didn't know any. With the exception of a Shakespeare intensive I took one summer at LAMDA in London, my training had been geared toward script analysis and performance for TV and film.

I reached out to my friend Stefan Haves. Stefan and I met while students at Cal State Northridge, before I dropped out to do *Falcon Crest*. He directs and teaches the art of clowning at places like Cirque Du Soleil. For seriously fun theater games, Stefan is your guy (send in the clown director—don't bother, he's here!). When we caught up, he said that one of our old college buddies, Bill Taylor, was now a professor in the theater department at Cal State. He urged me to call Bill. My dream was to teach at university level but for that you need a master's or a doctorate. Since I didn't even have a BA, I put that dream away. Before our meeting, I checked out the CSUN website and discovered I was on their VIP Alumna page. Little old dropout me!

Bill introduced me to the chair of the theater department, who was a fan. He offered me a spot teaching Introduction to Theater but I had to come clean: I sheepishly confessed that I'd never finished my bachelor's. He smiled and said, "People with your level of professional experience can sometimes be approved at lecturer status. Let me see what I can do."

The next day, he called and said, "You're in."

In less than a year, my private acting class was thriving. I taught two courses at CSUN. One of them was a dramatic literature course, where I was able to share my Shakespeare training. A student in my theater class was an actor and professional tango dancer. He wanted to be in my private acting class but couldn't afford the fee. It takes two to barter—I taught him acting, he taught me tango—and an obsession was born. For the next few years, I was a fixture at dance conventions and *milongas* (tango dance halls), and my passion gave birth to an idea for the book I spoke of earlier, *Shut Up and Dance.* At its core, *SUAD* was an exploration of masculine and feminine archetypes.

I mustered the courage to call my old shrink (*Death Cookie*)—guess who? I still wasn't making much money but my feet were on the ground for the first time that I could remember. I hadn't spoken to Stutz in years. Since archetypes are so much a part of his work, I thought that getting a few pithy, attributed Stutzian lines for *SUAD* would be apt. When I called, he mentioned that he was working on a book too, called *The Tools.* When *The Tools* became a bestseller, Stutz and coauthor Barry Michels began giving workshops. When Barry decided to do seminars on his own, I stepped in to help Stutz. Our collaboration led from assisting to teaching—a rich period of sinking deep into the work, learning not just for myself but for those to whom I would pass on the knowledge.

Stutz was generous and never proprietary when I brought a feminine perspective to *The Tools*, coming up with teaching strategies of my own. In the last few years, he has mostly retired from counseling, sending his overflow to me, for which I am deeply honored. In a circuitous journey from client to peer, we're now close friends. We talk almost every day.

When the walls of my world came crashing down—the Fall of the House (and Ego) of Rose—I thought my life was over.

Now, I feel it's when my most authentic life began.

~

"You can't think your way into right action,
but you can act your way into right thinking."
—Bill Wilson, founder of Alcoholic Anonymous

You can't be that kid standing at the top of the waterslide,
overthinking it. You have to go down the chute.
—Tina Fey

If the Spaghetti Sticks, Wear It

People at crossroads often ask, "When and how will I know what I'm *supposed to be doing*?"

It's impossible to know by *thinking* about it. The only way to find the answers is by getting into forward motion and taking action. Only then will your path reveal itself—the throw-spaghetti-at-the-wall-and-see-what-sticks approach.

My client Rebecca hated her longtime gig as a marketing executive. She'd saved enough that she could live without income for six months, even a year, if she was conservative. She had the luxury to quit her job but had no idea what the future looked like.

I gave her the following exercise.

JOURNALING EXERCISE
Musing

For the next two weeks, before you go to bed, write three to five things you might want to do with your life. Do it *quickly* and don't overthink. Let it be fun. Allow your subconscious to conjure whatever it conjures. The thoughts and ideas may be practical—or seem silly, unrealistic, even outlandish. Write them down.

Do not edit yourself.

Here's a prompt to help move you along:

Think of something you do that makes you lose track of time. An activity that's easy for you to become immersed in. Something you get paid for or one that you don't—but make it something you *enjoy*.

For example your first list might be:

Bookstore owner
Nonprofit fundraiser
Dog groomer
Vintage furniture dealer
Chef

Do the exercise each night—*but don't look at what you wrote the night before.*

Start fresh every time.

The next night's list might read:

Nonprofit Fundraiser
Knitting shop owner
Dog Groomer
Bookstore owner
Hospice worker

Do this every night for two weeks, without looking at what you wrote the night before.

At the end of those two weeks, go through your lists and write down the three things that repeat themselves the most. This will give you an idea of what your subconscious is yearning for.

The last list might read:

Knitting shop owner
Bookstore owner
Vintage furniture dealer

Now, make a list of actions you can take that allow you to investigate each idea.

For the list above, research every knitting shop, independent bookstore, and vintage furniture shop in your area. Go visit. Speak to the owners if you can. Talk to the people who work there. Have any of your friends been in those businesses? Ask them about their experience.

The above example is actually Rebecca's final list. After doing the groundwork, she had the courage to try out her dream. She found a charming, vacant storefront in her neighborhood and opened a shop that sold hand-dyed yarns. She started a class for knitting. The vintage furniture and knickknacks she sells are special, selected by her keen eye—as are the meticulously curated books. From the stress and demands of a marketing executive, she moved on to the joyful uncertainty of a new, authentic, nurturing life. She makes less money now, "But I do well enough. And love every minute of it."

She changed deadlines into lifelines.

~

Dreams become reality when we put our minds to it
and take action.
—Serena Williams

The Field
(of dreams)

Forward motion activates higher forces, even if you don't believe in them. That's what the mountaineer W. H. Murray was talking about when he spoke of commitment: "The moment one definitely commits oneself, then Providence moves too . . . A whole stream of events issues from the decision, raising in one's favor all manner of unforeseen incidents and meetings and material assistance, which no one could have dreamed would have come their way."

Stutz calls this phenomenon the Field.

The Mother is the archetypal force who reigns over the Field. She's the one who creates what Jung called synchronicity—happy coincidences. When you don't know which way to go, the Mother opens doors and says, "*This* is the way." But in order to help you, she needs to be able to *see* you. For this to happen, Stutz says that you must obey the 4 Laws of the Field: Nonattachment, Microtransactions, Commitment, and Self-Restraint.

Nonattachment

This means nonattachment to results—the Pre-Win described in the Laws of Action—but also nonattachment to preconceived ideas. A dear friend, the writer Hubert Selby Jr., used to tell me, "Give up the image and the vision will appear." My *image* was that the only way I could be happy was to be a successful actress. When life forced me to relinquish that idea, I discovered unforeseen skills and talents, and am happier now in my current work than I ever was as an actor.

Stutz talks about something he calls the String of Pearls. In a classic necklace, all the pearls are perfectly matched. They're the same size and coloration. If I work as an actor, or barista, or yoga teacher, writer, or coach, all of those roles are worth the same. I'm just showing up—just stringing pearls. This concept is about identity. Stutz says, "I'm not a winner, I'm not a loser. I'm just the guy who puts the next pearl on the string."

THE TOOL
Loss Processing
(P.S.)

Close your eyes. Imagine something you're attached to—a relationship, your career, your health. You may imagine it as an actual object attached to the branch of a tall tree. Hold on to it with both hands. You're hanging from it, legs dangling down. You feel an immense desire to continue to hold on. Make it feel like life or death.

In your mind, say the words, "I'm willing to lose everything".

Let go.

Now you're falling—but it's a gentle fall, a feeling of surrender. You feel a great sense of release. Of peace.

You look down and see that you're falling into the face of a brilliant, beautiful sun. As your body touches the face of this sun, it disintegrates and now you're a part of it. You feel yourself in a state of pure outflow, radiating golden light.

Then you notice there are hundreds—thousands—of other suns, as far as you can see. Their rays reach out to you and your rays reach toward them; you are connected. You are an integral part of this infinitely large, glowing, matrix of radiant suns.

Use this Tool anytime you feel too attached to something (like I was, to "actress")—your career, your Instagram account, what people think of you. You can also use it in a situation where you're afraid of being rejected or failing—at a job interview, public speaking, a romantic relationship. The Tool can also help you process a loss that's already happened.

The end of the Loss Processing Tool puts you in the world of Universe Two, a powerful space where you are whole and nothing is missing. We call this the Potency of Nonattachment. The paradox of being in a state of nonattachment is that it *empowers* you. Like savings in a spiritual bank account, it's the ultimate fuck-you money.

Microtransactions

Every person you come into contact with is a representative of the Field.

That's what the Hindu greeting namaste means—"I recognize the divine within you." There is no hierarchy (see Universe One) among us. We are all worth the same, each a pearl on the necklace of humanity. When you treat each person you meet with kindness and interest and make them feel valued, you're obeying the law of Microtransactions. This creates a positive culture in the cosmology of life and connects you with the Field.

The law of Microtransactions also means that if we hold on to resentments, justified or not, our forward motion gets blocked. This doesn't mean we have to endorse those who have wronged us. But if we want to connect fully with the Field, we cannot afford to nurture ill will.

THE TOOL
Active Love
(P.S. & B.M.)[7]

Close your eyes and think of a person you have a resentment toward.

Imagine they're sitting about ten feet away, facing you.

Now, as in the Radiation tool, feel a presence of infinite love all around you. Bring that presence into your heart.

There, it begins to expand, but instead of spilling back out into the room, concentrate all that love—that intensely

[7] Not to relive my own trauma, but this is the Tool I was teaching at the Saturday Night Massacre. Also, with Stutz and Barry's consent, I've changed the wording from the way it is written in the Tools book.

benevolent energy—into a beam of golden light. Sent it from your heart directly into the center of the other person's chest.

Hold nothing back.

When the love enters the other person, don't just watch, feel *it enter—as if you are traveling along with the beam of Infinite Love.*

You feel a sense a oneness with them. You are connected in love. All resentment is gone.

Commitment

We always need to be in a committed state—not only to a certain goal, but committed *to commitment itself.* This is what keeps us moving forward. The committed state has nothing to do with external achievements; that's Universe One material. Universe Two, the realm of the Divine Feminine, is ceaselessly creative and constantly evolving. When we make commitments and keep them, we align ourselves with the awesome power of that universe.

A commitment can be as simple as writing in our journals each day or waking up at a set time. The simple act of follow-through on the commitments we've made gives us a confidence we cannot experience in any other way. It's an indicator that we have mastery over our will. Sometimes the idea of personal will gets a bad rap; it's often characterized as stubbornness and literal willfulness. (In recovery groups, the much-used phrase is "self-will run riot.") But as we learn to use our will properly, it becomes a valuable asset and essential ally in achieving our highest potential. Making commitments and keeping them is one of the most powerful ways to strengthen our force of will.

A favorite story of mine is one Stutz tells about a young boxer and his coach. The coach tells the boxer that they're going to start training every day at five a.m. The boxer says that five a.m. is too early, he'd rather start at six. The coach answers, "If you don't have the will to get up to train at five a.m., you won't have the will to get up before a ten-count."

THE TOOL
The Jet Stream
(P.S.)

Close your eyes. Start by feeling an extreme heaviness in your body. You feel tired. Intensify that feeling of exhaustion.

Now, feel the presence of a forward-moving, infinitely powerful stream of energy that exists on a much higher plane than the one that your physical body inhabits. This is the Jet Stream, a powerful current of air circling the globe several miles above the earth.

Your goal is to connect to that force. The way you do this is by feeling a strong desire to be lifted up by its powerful energy.

Make no physical effort. Just keep focused on the desire to join the force above your head. You feel yourself rising. As you are lifted, you become part of the dynamic, all-powerful stream of energy above. Your physical body dissolves into that formidable flow.

Now there is no more effort required—in fact, there is no more You. *You are part of this unstoppable force of forward-motion energy. You have entered the Jet Stream.*

Another version of this Tool is to imagine an action or task you've committed to. Place the image of that action or task into the Jet Stream. When you feel yourself rise up and enter the Jet Stream, see yourself doing the action or task with newfound energy and determination.

Self-Restraint

Self-restraint means abstinence from all addictions. The usual ones are drugs and alcohol, gambling, sex and love, eating, and spending. But there are subtler addictions—such as worry, anxiety, self-attack, negativity, and issues of control.

When you're practicing an addiction, it is impossible to move forward—it's like putting a cork in the bottle of your full actualization. I once asked a client with food issues, "What are you hungry for? What are you really seeking?" I already knew the answer: spiritual connection. Living in a perpetual state of addiction is the opposite of living in the grace of forward motion; stagnant and primitive, addiction detaches us from the sacred. Nothing of value can be created from this state. In order to be a creator—to live one's life in unity with and awareness of the Field—one must abstain from all addictions.

Only then can we gain access to an unlimited source of fertile, dynamic, and creative energy.

THE TOOL
Embodiment
(P.S. & J.R.)

Close your eyes. Think of a time you felt compelled to act on a negative impulse or addiction.

You had a strong desire to overeat, to gamble, to waste time on social media, to rage about some years-old incident where you felt slighted.

Relive this feeling of acute craving.

Now, imagine this craving as an aura of tiny Xs just outside your body. The X-filled aura has a frenzied, desperate quality. It grows larger and larger as it moves outward, hungrily searching for satisfaction.

From deep inside you, a voice yells, "Enough!"

Suddenly, everything stops.

The Xs calm, then uncross, becoming simple lines of energy that begin to drift down and enter your body. (Think of flakes in a snow globe, slowly drifting to the bottom after being shaken.)

Inside your body and around your abdomen, the lines organize themselves into a grid or latticelike pattern.

This pattern is the organized fabric of the entire universe, of which you are a holistic part. Connected to this larger whole, you feel a profound sense of stillness and connection.

You have everything you need because you are *everything you need.*

~

I've talked a lot about the archetype of the Mother. She holds creativity, flow, and life force. In the next chapter, we'll explore another archetype, one that embodies structure, life lessons, and Time.

Take a breath before we meet the Father.

Chapter Eight

The Father

The father is the guiding principle,
the bringer of law and structure.
He does not merely protect,
he compels the soul to grow.
—Rainer Maria Rilke

A father is a cliff you break yourself against in order to
Become the shape of yourself.
—James Hillman

The Father, or Divine Masculine archetype, is ancient as myth itself. While the Mother—the Divine Feminine—nurtures life, the Father builds *containers* for it to thrive.

He is the holder of form.

Before we go any further, I want to say that I'm aware that the masculine energetic has attributes that appear conventionally patriarchal. At first glance, this archetype might present as controversial. But I'm not talking about the Father as culture has distorted him—rigid, angry, detached, domineering—I mean a force existing *outside* the parameters of social constructs. When I speak of the Father, I'm referring to what Carl Jung called the *animus*, a contrasexual archetype that, like the *anima*, or feminine aspect, resides within the psyche of every human being. It is an energy available to all, regardless of gender identity. Masculine and feminine energies are dynamic polarities, like inhale and exhale, day and night, sun and moon. When in complete expression of individual personhood, there's fluidity—a dance between feminine and masculine principles.

In such full expression, there *is* no polarity, only union and wholeness.

In discussing the Masculine energetic, I ask you to suspend judgment. In doing so, you will more readily engage with the hard, transcendent work of exploring the sacred.

~

By default, our impulse is to conjure the Father as human, to give it the face of our own father—or for those who never met that man, to project onto the archetype our ideas and experiences about stepfathers, imagined fathers, mentors, etcetera. *But the archetypal Father is not human.* He is a force beyond our limited consciousness and perception. The archetype of the Father embodies authority, discipline, life lessons, initiatory experiences, and structure; he rules Time and Space. In Judeo-Christian traditions, he is often depicted as the old man in the sky with the long white beard; in stories and films, he is Gandalf from *The Lord of the Rings*, King T'Chaka from *Black Panther*, Mufasa from *The Lion King*, Star *Wars'* Obi-Wan Kenobi (and his dark side, Darth Vader). We also know him as the black-cloaked figure with the scythe—Death—the ultimate image of our mortality.

There is much to say about this archetype. But right now, I ask you to pick your own image—again, not your actual father, but one that symbolizes a personal reflection of the qualities of the best version of the Father force: wise, benevolent, self-sacrificing, and strong.

EXERCISE
The Father
(J.R.)

Close your eyes and try to visualize an image of the archetypal Father force.

Allow yourself to be creative here. For some, he may look human. Others will summon Zeus or the Chinese deity Shangdi or the Yoruba god Shango. He might be an amalgam from myths, movies, and books—King Arthur or Heracles. He could be a real-world person like Martin Luther King Jr. or even Anthony Hopkins.

You have freedom to depart from that kind of anthropomorphic imagery by seeing him as a bolt of lightning crackling across a black, stormy sky or as a radiant life-giving sun. If not visually inclined, you may experience him as a scent—leather or sandalwood—or a beautiful piece of music: Bach, Gershwin, the Foo Fighters "My Hero," or Puccini's "Nessum Dorma." It doesn't matter how literal or non-literal the image is.

What matters is that you can feel him.

~

As with the Mother archetype, some of my clients are resistant to this exercise. They had fathers who were distant, absent, angry, critical, physically violent—or they never knew their fathers at all. Like so many of us who feel squashed under the heel of a male-dominated society, they're mistrustful of men and suspect of masculine energy. But please remember—*every* human being has a primal connection to the archetypal Father. He's an essential part of our full actualization, the Yang to the Yin.

To reject him is to reject a part of ourselves.

Daddy's Girl

My own father was tall and handsome, the quintessential leading man. His booming, old-style baritone voice—"legit" as they call it in the business—was almost operatic. Think John Raitt or Robert Goulet. (Ask ChatGPT!) In the days before tiny mics, those singers needed big voices in order to be heard in the back row of auditoriums and amphitheaters. Back then, Dad did summer stock, playing the love interest to aging musical stars like Jane Powell, Jane Russell, and Chita Rivera (I *said*, ask ChatGPT).

As a child, I watched from the wings as he played Curly in *Oklahoma!*—sauntering onstage in full cowboy regalia, he serenaded Laurie about his "pretty little surrey with the fringe on top." As the dashing, sword and doublet-clad Sir Lancelot in *Camelot*, he swore his undying love to Queen Guinevere. As Skye Masterson in *Guys and Dolls,* Dad rocked a sexy pinstripe suit and cocky fedora, blew on a pair of dice, and sang "Luck Be a Lady." After each showstopping number, applause shook the room. And how's this for bigger than life: I'm four years old, in the audience with Mom and Stevie while Dad plays the tragic carnival barker Billy Bigelow in *Carousel*. He belts out the famous "Soliloquy," announcing to the world that he'll do whatever it takes to provide for his unborn daughter. "I'll go out and make it, or steal it, or take it, or die!" Crowned in a halo of light, my father seemed to float in the air like a god. After the show, he took me in his arms and said, "*You're* the one I was singing to."

The roar of the Daddy Issues, the smell of the crowd.

By the time he hit his forties, his career was at standstill. Instead of floating above the stage, he hid out in Fresno, working for a relative's home improvement business. He didn't want to get a day job in LA because he was afraid of risking a run-in with actors and agents that he knew—a fate even worse than showbiz death. (I came to know that feeling well: *Shazam!*) He told Stevie and me that he was just helping his uncle out for a while, but "a while" lasted years. In the time before the family relocated to Fresno, he was rarely home. Mom performed the duties of both father and mother—and worked during the day as well. Dad was hopeless at math (like his daughter) so Mom was the one who encouraged my genius baby brother; she helped with science class projects and took him to Boy Scout jamborees and toy car racing derbies. Mom was the handyman; she hung the bookshelves and fixed broken appliances. Even when he was back, if there was any kind of emergency, she was the one who dealt with it. It was always that way. As a toddler, I split open my chin when I fell off my hobbyhorse. Dad threw the toy against the wall then called Mom at work to ask her what to do. She screamed over the phone, "Take her to the emergency room!" When I was twelve, I fell off my bike and split my chin again (see a pattern? I break falls with my face—still do), he called Reta at work and . . . *Take her to the emergency room!* Mom filed the taxes, paid the bills, and had a deep understanding of the VCR. Because of her, they eventually got their finances together.

When I began working with Stutz, the only model I had for the Father archetype was Reta.

Dad was my playmate, ally, and champion—I adored him. But sometimes I longed for the structure that a cliched '50s sitcom *Father Knows Best* type would provide. A dad who worked nine to five. A dad in a tweed jacket with suede elbow patches who smoked a pipe and explained the difference between Index funds and ETFs to me while building a gazebo in the backyard. When I do the Father exercise, I literally see Gregory Peck as Atticus Finch in *To Kill a Mockingbird*—in black and white, as he was in the film.

The opposite of my beloved, Technicolor song-and-dance man dad.

Point being, not only do you not have to use the father you grew up with, but you get to customize your version of the archetype, one you can access whenever you need it.

~

> Nothing else matters except sitting down every day and trying.
> —Steven Pressfield, *The War of Art*

> Creativity is not a talent. It's a way of operating.
> You keep showing up, and sometimes the muse shows up too.
> —Rosanne Cash

The Plane of Will

One of the ways to get close to the Father archetype is through structured action.

You do that by making daily commitments to yourself and fulfilling those commitments. Once you've done this consistently over a period of time, you begin to feel like you're living on a different level of existence. Stutz calls it the Plane of Will. When you're on the Plane of Will, you feel a sense of momentum, confidence, and personal power.

You're living in the domain of the Father.

The key to engaging with the Plane of Will is to start small. The idea of running a mile can be daunting, but can you commit to running a single block each day? If that's too much, how about half a block? No? Then what about just putting on running shoes and walking outside? Make the commitment as small as you need it to be. The important thing is to *keep* that commitment.

No matter what.

I asked my client Suzanne to commit to spending fifteen minutes a day on her book. I told her that she didn't even have to write. She could simply open a Word document and play with the font. Of course, she could work longer if she wished—but fifteen minutes got the gold star. The payoff was twofold.

Following through on a commitment builds inner confidence; and, by developing the habit of entering Book World each day, her subconscious would begin to provide ideas.

Father Time

The simple act of making small commitments and keeping them will put you on the Plane of Will. To kick it up a notch, add the element of Time.

The archetypal feminine relationship to Time is cyclical and eternal in nature. The Greek goddess Persephone, in her seasonal cycles between the under- and overworld, is an example of this expression. The classic Death figure, a skeleton with black cloak and scythe, represents the linear—we are born (the beginning) and we die (the end). In its masculine form, Time is associated with linear progression. When you commit on Sunday to doing something on Monday—and keep that commitment—you create a link between those days that can be depicted as a horizontal line. By adding a specific time to show up (say, 9 a.m., for fifteen minutes), you're making a sacrifice at the altar of the Father.

You're *giving* him that time—that chunk of your life.

Stutz likes to tell the story of two piano players who get to the conservatory at 10 a.m. on a Monday morning. They practice the same piece of music with the same level of virtuosity for the same amount of time. The difference is that Player One decided on Sunday night that she would begin her practice on Monday at 10 a.m. Player Two got there at 10 a.m. to practice because she *felt* like it. If you want to align yourself with the power of the Father, aspire to be Player One.

Time is the ultimate currency.

You have a certain number of days and hours in your life—what do you want to do with them?

~

Before me lies a mass of shapeless days;
They are coming, they will pass;
And I shall weave them into a pattern, and call it life.
—Amy Lowell

The Giant Pearl

In the last chapter, I mentioned Stutz's concept of the String of Pearls. When Player One does the one-hour practice she committed to, it doesn't matter how badly or how well she plays; after each session, another pearl is added to the strand. The mistake we often make is to believe that once we achieve a certain goal—a book is written, a business established, the ideal fat-to-muscle ratio obtained—we've won. The necklace is finished, resplendent for all to see.

The ultimate jeweler, Madame X, tells us so.

Society promotes the fantasy that if our kid gets into *this* school, if we have *this* many followers on IG, well, all's right with the world. This is called an outer motivation system. But in that system, only two things can happen: We don't get what we want and become demoralized—or we get what we want and soon find out our "high" is short-lived. On the Plane of Will, we're *inwardly* motivated. No matter the result, we're going to keep putting pearls on the string.

This makes us unstoppable.

Fake Forward Motion

Suzanne was a successful screenwriter. After retiring, she had an idea for a novel but couldn't get herself to work on it. She hadn't written anything for a year.

"Jamie, I don't understand . . . I'm *disciplined*—but I just can't find the time to write!"

"Tell me about your typical day," I asked.

"Well . . . I have a strict self-care routine. I wake up at six thirty a.m. and meditate for twenty minutes. Then I do a ninety-minute yoga practice followed by a cold plunge. I get dressed and make a smoothie and by then it's around ten a.m. That's when my daughter drops off the grandkids."

"Every day?" She nodded. "For how long?"

"They're with me until she gets off work around five."

"You babysit."

"And I *love* it."

"Your family comes first. I get it. You love those kids and you're helping your daughter. But right now in your life, what's the most important thing? For *you.*"

There was no hesitation: "My writing."

"Hmm. So, where does writing fit in with your 'self-care' routine?" I saw a switch flip in her eyes. "It might be time to do a cold plunge—into your pages!"

One of Madame X's cleverest tools is to convince us that something *else* is more important than pursuing our deepest yearnings. Stutz calls this Fake Forward Motion. MX convinced Suzanne that exercise and meditation took precedence over working on her novel. There's an old adage that says "Writers have the cleanest houses"—that's because most of them would rather do anything than face a blank page. Suzanne's good faith morning practice *seemed* righteously motivated; moving the body is essential. But not at the cost of being idle in creative realms that nourish us.

Rituals can easily become obstacles in disguise.

JOURNALING EXERCISE
The Plane of Will

Each night before going to sleep, journal about the next day and write down the three most important things you want to accomplish. Do it in order of importance.

For Suzanne it might look like this:

Work on book
Meditate
Yoga

Since her yoga and meditation practice helps her enter a creative place, she may choose to do those things first. But she needs to *measure her time* (Father archetype) to allow space to write. She can also alternate days for certain practices. She can mix it up.

A typical day might now look like this:

6:30–8:00 Meditation, yoga
8:00 to 9:00 or 9:30 Write
10:00 Grandkids

After a week or so of the new, improved morning practice, she started regaining her writer's confidence. Suzanne ended up shortening her other practices so she'd have more time to work on her novel. As of now, she's halfway through the first draft and I have no doubt—*if* she stays on the Plane of Will—that she'll finish. Madame X will always be there on the sidelines, but Suzanne has the Tools to keep her at bay.

~

> You don't have a right to the cards
> you believe you should have been dealt.
> You have an obligation to play the hell out
> of the ones you're holding.
> —Cheryl Strayed

The Gift of Adversity

Like the Mother, the Father is a loving force. You are his precious child. He cares about only one thing—your personal evolution. To ensure that evolution, he will create events in your life that demand you push past what you think you're capable of.

For millennia, the role of the Father has been to initiate us into adulthood. In ancient tribal cultures, initiation was done through sacred ritual that often involved a test of physical endurance like fasting, isolation, and scarification. (The feminine force also provides initiatory experiences, which we'll discuss in the next chapter.) In modern culture, initiation isn't provided by a tribal elder but by the events and happenings of our lives. Orchestrated by the Father, their purpose is to propel us into spiritual growth.

If you cannot *accept* an event, you're rejecting the Father. Expanding on that, Stutz calls another of his concepts the Philosophy of Events. The Philosophy of Events attests that adverse happenings are *supposed* to occur; they're not indicators that something is "wrong" with you. Embedded in every negative event is an opportunity. Developing spiritual skills to navigate such encounters is more important than getting a good result.

When bad things happen (things that feel unfair, unexpected or harmful), it's important that we accept our fate. Although it can be hard to see at the time, what we interpret as defeats or disappointments, even illnesses, all have their place and purpose. From the Father's point of view, it's precisely the most difficult events that make us grow. As painful as they are, such happenings provide initiation into spiritual maturity. Such maturity has nothing to do with age because many undergo initiatory experiences when young. Some are compelled to overcome adversity; others are mangled or destroyed by it. Why is one person able to adapt and another not? Each of us has their own path. The "maturity" is in *how* we respond to adversity. And for that, we need faith.

But faith in what?

At the human, non-god level of consciousness, we cannot know the answer to that question. To have faith is a *decision*. (It takes faith to have faith.) I see *faith* as an unflinching attitude of acceptance that forces us to deeply probe the experience of something that is seemingly negative in order to transmute it into the positive. This is less challenging when facing the mundane frustrations of life—you get sick while on holiday, your kid has their first heartbreak—but what about the bigger events? What about bankruptcy, death, illness?

How do we accept the unacceptable?

~

There's no people like show people,
they smile when they are low
Yesterday they told you you would not go far
That night you open and there you are
Next day on your dressing room they've hung a star
Let's go on with the show
Let's go on with the show
—Irving Berlin, "There's No Business Like Show Business"

In his early seventies, out of the blue, Dad got a great role in a show that starred the married comedy veterans Joseph Bologna and Renée Taylor. By the end of the first week of rehearsals, he had learned the script of the entire show. He was always the first to the theater and the last to leave. "Bermuda Avenue Triangle" turned out to be a hit and played to packed houses every night during its LA run. The troupe went on the road and it was just like the old days. *Back in the biz!* He would call from his hotel room to say how much the audience loved the show. He was so damn happy.

Shortly into the tour, odd things began to happen.

The old pro Stewart Rose was forgetting his lines. One night, he showed up for the second act in the wrong costume. When they moved on to the next leg of the tour, they cut him loose. Not long after, the handsome, super-fit, charismatic baritone was diagnosed with Alzheimer's. The man who came of age in the sharp-dressed Sy Devore Rat Pack era grew soft-bodied and sloppy. As the disease progressed, his ambitions faded as well. His lifelong shame at never having become a famous singer mercifully vanished.

It broke my heart, but still provided a gift.

The dementia's progression distilled his essence into a message-in-a-bottle of warm, funny, loving father. We spent Tuesdays together to give Reta a break; I called it Daddy Day Care. We'd make pilgrimages to our old haunt, Patys, where black-and-white headshots of famous actors like John Wayne and Elizabeth Taylor graced the walls, along with folks who had their fifteen seconds of walk-on fame—or their fifteen commercials, or their three seasons on TV—most of them now forgotten. He searched the headshots looking for faces he worked with back in the day. When his eyes alit on an old chum, he'd say a vibrant "Hello!" He loved talking to *real* people in the restaurant too. It was fun and funny—at first—but as the disease worsened, he could be unpredictable and inappropriate. He would tell someone they had great hair or a great smile, following the compliment with the ever-charming, "Would you like to see my penis?" *Yikes.* I'd do a quick, apologetic song and dance and once they understood his impairment, they were lovely.

After one of those awkward improvs, I remember steering him out of the place *fast*. We held hands—the only way I could prevent him from wandering off—and when we got outside, a homeless guy put his hand out, “Got any change?”

Dad whispered, “I don’t give him money right?”

“That’s right, Dad.”

I did some more steering and when we got to the car, he hesitated, glancing back, then pulled a dollar bill from his wallet.

“I’m going to go give him this.”

I watched nervously from the car as he handed over the buck.

Dad was smiling when he came back. “I’m glad I did that!” he said, adding, “Oh! I forgot to tell you—I had a talk with God this morning.”

“Really? And what did God say?” (I hoped there wouldn’t be a penis joke.)

“He said, ‘Stewie? Give a dollar to someone who needs it.’”

~

You must go on.
I can’t go on.
I’ll go on.
—Samuel Beckett, *The Unnamable*

I used to have nightmares about my father getting so sick that Mom and I would no longer be able to care for him at home.

My worst fears finally came true.

A gall bladder infection sent him to the hospital, where he was sedated then catheterized. Mom was wiped out so I sent her home and stayed overnight. I didn't sleep because he kept trying to pull out the catheter. When I held his hands to stop him, he cried, "Jamie it hurts! It hurts! Let go of my hands, give me my hands!" After that long, brutal, awful night, Mom and I met with his doctors. They said they could take out his gall bladder but the operation would probably make his Alzheimer's symptoms worse. Treated or untreated, he was heading nowhere good. We nixed the operation and told them to treat the infection with antibiotics. Because we didn't have the money for the twenty-four-hour nursing he required, they transferred him to a nursing care facility.

Mom and I knew that was his last stop.

Even with a turkey that you know will fold
You may be stranded out in the cold
But still you wouldn't change it for a sack of gold
Let's go on with the show!

But there was no sack of gold and the show was closing.

The nursing home was a seventy-five-hundred-a-month shithole. Medi-Cal wouldn't kick in until Mom had exhausted their modest savings. Dad was put in a tiny, shared room with a thin curtain separating him from his neighbor. There was just enough space for his narrow hospital bed and a small nightstand. I had read somewhere that it's important for the caretaking staff to understand who their patient *was*—that they had a life, that they are loved, and worthy of respect and dignity. I bought a CD player so they could listen to his songs—his *voice*—and showed them photos of how he looked back in the day. One of the orderlies said, "He's fly." But another made me stop because apparently the noise was bothering his roommate.

The horror was, he was still "there" enough to know that he wasn't home. He kept pleading, "*Get me out of here!* I want to go home!" Each time he said it was like a stab.

A few days later, Mom got a call from the place at midnight.

"He's going crazy!" said the nurse. "You have to get over here!"

Luckily, it was only a ten-minute drive. Reta stayed with him and I took over in the morning. Mom was eighty years old, and I didn't know how much of this she could take. I told the staff to call me instead when he got agitated. The next night, my cell rang around 8 p.m. Someone was telling me, "Please come!"—I could hear Dad bellowing in the background. "Reta!" he shouted. "Reta!" I spent hours trying to calm him down.

This became a nightly ritual.

Ten days later, Stutz asked me to help with a weekend seminar that he and Barry Michels were doing at the Omega Institute in Rhinebeck, New York. Given Dad's condition, I didn't want to travel but Mom insisted. "This is *important*, Jamie. You have to live your life."

The day before I left, I spent a long afternoon alone with Dad.

Dad: "You're the best daughter I ever had." (*I'm the only daughter he ever had.*)
Me: "You're the best father I ever had."
Dad: "You love me!"

Me: "Yes, I do, Daddy."

Dad: (*putting his hands on my cheeks*) "I love this face. This is my face." (*pause*) "You're Jamie right?"

Me: "Yes, Daddy. I'm Jamie."

Dad: "You're my daughter?"

Me: "I'm your daughter."

Dad: "Oh, good."

I was in touch with Mom the whole weekend that I was away. On the drive back to Manhattan with Phil and Barry to catch my flight back to LA, I got the news. After hanging up, I softly said aloud, as if to myself, "My father died." They didn't try to "fix" the situation in any way and held space for me to grieve. I sobbed and they had no words, which in that moment were the very best kind. What better place to be in the face of such a cosmic, primal bulletin? Alone with two of the best shrinks in the world.

How blessed was I.

How blessed to have been on so much of my father's long, beautiful journey.

As you might imagine, I wondered, *Why was I not there with him when he passed?* Why did I listen to my mother? Why didn't I just *stay*? But like so many things in life, there was mystical timing at work. Time and timing are in the realm of the archetypal Father. It was perfect that I wasn't there—it was just him and Mom.

Reta, his first love. His bride of almost sixty years.

The moment was for them only.

I knew just what he would want for his funeral—

A *show*!

I spent the flight home cutting together a Farewell Tour movie on my laptop—photos of him as boy and during his heyday as a performer—dapper Dad and ravishing Reta in costume from various shows . . . shots of them with me and Stevie when we were babies, getting bigger straight through adulthood. I even had video of him performing a showstopping number from "Victory Canteen," a musical he did in the seventies. In the car on the way to the chapel, I was *still* editing. At the end of the screening, everyone leapt to their feet. I never cried and smiled so hard in my life. In her eulogy, Reta said, "My husband taught me how to love the world—and I'll never forgive him for that."

That night, the apartment felt beyond empty; it was Stewart Rose–less. Dad's worn-out recliner sat forlornly in front of the television and all of his meds still lined the counter. The tuxedos he performed in hung in the closet like skeletons. Family portraits spanning the decades dotted the living room, but the only one I saw was Dad.

He was everywhere, but nowhere.

Mom studied each picture, as if at a museum. Her fingers caressed the wedding ring she now wore around her neck. She turned to me and said, "I can't believe he's gone."

In the patter between songs during his club acts, he used to say how much he loved us—me and Stevie and Reta. "I'm a family man," he'd say. This is what we put on the headstone:

Stewart Rose
5/25/1932–5/29/2017
A Family Man

All philosophy begins in wonder.
—Plato

Radical Acceptance

There's great mystery in the power of the archetypal Father—the Divine Masculine energetic. That force knows what should happen, *not* the human being. The task of being human is to *accept* whatever's happening, and stand squarely in the present moment.

To be in a state of what Stutz calls Radical Acceptance.

Most of the time, when people believe they've accepted something, all they've done is learned to tolerate it. But that kind of acceptance is simply resignation. Radical Acceptance is an unflinching, full-bodied, *felt* experience that requires a total surrender of ego and judgement. You have to give up the belief that you know what should or shouldn't happen.

What's good or bad. What's "fair"—

The history of civilization tells us that trying to extract fairness from the world is a losing game. Regardless of your opinion, events relentlessly *happen*. Keeping one's sanity in a mad, mad world requires an enthusiastic jump into a state of what I like to call I-don't-know-ness—or *I-can't-know-ness*. In other words, a state of wonder. Wonder embodies awe and amazement. Wonder describes the feeling of being overcome during a magnificent sunset or while watching the exquisitely stylized mating dance of swans. Radical Acceptance is a profound state of wonder—the joy of being alive to witness the Mystery unfolding before you.

THE TOOL
RADICAL ACCEPTANCE
(P.S.)

Close your eyes and think of a situation or event that you judge as negative. In your mind say the words, "This should not be happening."

Imagine yourself taking three steps back from the event—not ordinary steps, but God-sized steps. Your view expands to include the entire Universe. This is the point of view of the Father. Silently say, or simply feel, the word "Perfect."

When you do, you'll feel *something—a tremendous force. The Father has appeared.*

You feel humility and awe in his presence. Joy infuses your body. You feel a sense of celebration that such a force is making itself known in your life.

You've been chosen to have this experience.

~

When using the Radical Acceptance Tool, it isn't the event you're celebrating—the "happening"—but the presence of the Father force itself. *An attitude of radical acceptance does not mean passivity.* The Tool simply allows you to detach from ego-driven fears and judgements so that you gain the clarity to define what actions, if any, can be taken.

A few years ago, I was angry about something *political.* I spent hours on Facebook ranting and raving about my views (I know, I know)—which, courtesy of the wonderful world of algorithm, were mostly seen only by those who already agreed with me. I was ranting and raving to the choir. Still, when the dust settled and the results were in (in ways I did *not* approve of!), I had a realization: Acting out on social media was worse than doing nothing. Why? Because the futile exhibitionism made me *feel* like I was actually doing something. It was another version of Fake Forward Motion. If I had practiced Radical Acceptance and surrendered to the reality that there were vast amounts of people in my country with opinions other than my own, I might have been able to align with that calm, steady, wise part of myself—the Father energetic. Arriving at a cooler middle ground would at least have given me a fighting chance to decide what effective, real-world actions I could have taken.

~

> To be great is to be misunderstood.
> —Ralph Waldo Emerson

Sometimes it's easier to accept an event we don't like than what we judge to be a person's bad behavior. As an example, whether our perception is accurate or not, when we feel that someone has attacked us personally, it's painful. We tend to believe there can be no reason for such an affront because of the illusion that we are essentially good; hence, should be loved by everyone. Often, being "misunderstood" is harder to tolerate than being actively disliked. If we've done something wrong and are called out on it—even harshly—we can usually accept the unpleasant result as a consequence. But when we believe that we haven't committed a wrong and have been falsely accused, it's difficult to accept. We're hooked. If we could only get them to *understand* us, to see the logic behind our motives and even *appreciate* our side of the encounter, then we'd have a shot at convincing them to think well of us.

It's not by chance that people pay great sums for algorithms that increase their "likes" exponentially; we're wired for it.

THE TOOL
Hatred and Misunderstanding
(P.S.)

See the perpetrator. Say in your mind, "I accept your presence!"

The perpetrator vanishes and The Father appears, brandishing a sword of light.

In your mind, say to him, "I accept your gift!"

The Father rushes forward, plunges the sword into your chest, and disappears.

Say the words, "I accept my power"— grab the hilt of the sword and pull it out of your chest.

Hold the glowing sword above your head. Its radiance infuses every cell of your being.

You are now embodied with the wisdom and grounded strength of The Father force.

Some of us may be uncomfortable with the imagery of the sword—especially in the hands of a masculine figure. Here's an alternate version of the Tool:

See the perpetrator. Say in your mind, "I accept your presence!"

The perpetrator vanishes and The Father appears, holding a shining globe of light.

In your mind, say to him, "I accept your gift!"

The Father strides forward, places the glowing object in your hands and disappears.

Say the words, "I accept my power."

Hold the luminous globe over your head.

Its radiance infuses every cell of your being.

You are now embodied with the wisdom and grounded strength of The Father force.

Chapter Nine

Radical Forgiveness, Loss, and the Sick Shadow

Resentment is like drinking poison and waiting for the other person to die.
—Carrie Fisher

I forgave the Nazis, not because they deserved it, but because I deserved it.
—Eva Mozes Kor, *Letter of Forgiveness*

Radical Forgiveness

Resentment has no value. It does nothing to punish its target and severs our connection to the vitality and *nowness* of the present moment.

The only person it harms is us.

I resented my mother for decades. Resentment was my friend, my advisor, my savior. I'd loved her so much when I was little, but when she became abusive, I forged a hard, protective shell around my heart. Long after she stopped drinking and transformed herself into the loving mother I'd longed for, I kept stoking my hatreds. The poison seeped into all of my relationships. As an adult, the "asset" that helped me survive my childhood became a crippling, self-lacerating liability. When I experienced any kind of intimacy, my sharp tongue and judgmental attitude was like barbed wire guarding an abandoned house.

When I considered my mother's lineage, I had a revelation of compassion—the shell of anger began to crack. Reta's side of the family was rife with alcoholism. Her brother had overdosed on booze and pills when he was sixty-one, and her mother died of the same disease at forty-seven. Mom's father once beat her so badly that a neighbor called the police. She fled home at seventeen, met Dad at eighteen, and married at nineteen. With only the worst role models as parenting examples, she had me at twenty-two. The miracle is that she did something *none* of the alcoholics in her family were able to—she got sober and became the mother that she never had. If I'd kept my "justifiable" resentment going, I would never have been able to accept that gift.

Yet, anger can be important as well. Anger is often what motivates us to distance ourselves from those who mistreat us; in that way, anger is useful and healing. A question might arise: Is forgiveness or understanding even necessary?

I believe it is. It's not good for the spirit or the body to have one's heart barricaded; the heart is meant to be open and joyous. To lock it up is nothing short of tragic. In a sense, we end up treating our own hearts in the same way as did the perpetrators of violence and emotional abuse. But *how* do we forgive? How do we accept and embody the life-giving gift of forgiveness?

The universe is in a perpetual state of outflow. Forever expanding, it's always in forward motion. If we seek a vibrantly connected and productive life, it's essential to align ourselves with the energy of the cosmos. We too must be in ceaseless forward motion. Hatred, judgment, and resentment subvert and inhibit that desire.

I want to stress that forgiveness has nothing to do with condoning malignant acts; it is forgiveness that such acts occurred at all. In the last chapter, I spoke of initiation by the Father, or the Divine Masculine energetic. The Mother also provides such experiences and in some ways her initiation is even more powerful than the Father force. It is a step beyond radical acceptance and requires great sacrifice. If the Father allows us to radically accept events and people, the Divine Feminine energetic takes that acceptance even further:

Into radical *forgiveness.*

~

Judy was despondent.

She'd practiced the Tools and done her Shadow work but was still anchored in anxiety and negativity. After a few months, she told me, "No matter what potential happiness presents itself, I push it away. *I find fault.* I always feel like I'm on the outside looking in."

In his mid-forties, Judy's father died in a plane crash. She idolized him. She was fourteen. He was a successful businessman but when he died, the secret came out: he was drowning in debt. Her mom was forced to move with Judy and her brother from their opulent home into a cramped, rented apartment in the so-called slums of Beverly Hills, south of Wilshire Boulevard. Judy still went to Beverly High, but she was now one of the poor kids. Her rich friends never ostracized her, but she could feel the sting of class divides and winced when she imagined them talking behind her back: *She's so pathetic. If that happened to me, I would have killed myself.* Her mother got work as a saleswoman at Saks, which made things worse. When the clique of rich girls came into the store—the clique she was once a part of—they always asked for her mom to ring them up. They'd be on shopping sprees—paid for with their parents' credit cards.

Now, at the age of thirty-two, Judy had a great job and was about to get married. But she was tormented by fantasies of all the ways that life could take a sudden, unexpected turn that would leave her shamed, ruined, and distraught. She loved her job . . . but was that job right for her? She loved her fiancé . . . but once they got married, would the little things about him that irritated her eventually snowball into an avalanche of contempt?

What if I die young (like her father), *never having done what I was meant to?*

In her head, she was still living on the wrong side of Wilshire—with her roommate, Madame X.

During a session, I said, "It's like you're hiding in the bomb shelter that you built when you were a kid. The shelter helped you survive the war of grief and trauma after your father died, but the problem is that you've become a prisoner of that shelter. The war is *over*, Judy, but Madame X has you convinced that it never ended. She's dropping leaflets saying, "Never surrender!" Losing your Dad in the way that you did was a horrible tragedy. Look, we know how the story of life ends: in death, both natural and unnatural. That story is full of other endings too—friendships, jobs, romances—both natural and unnatural. Madame X *will* keep encouraging you to hide. She'll keep sending ammunition boxes marked 'Judy's War.' MX will bully you. She'll say, 'You've tried it *all*, Judy, and *everything failed*—the coaching with Jamie, The Tools, connecting with your 'Shadows' . . . *none* of it's ever going to work!' If you say, 'You're right. You win,' then the enemy you're surrendering to is *Madame X. Then* what? What have you actually gained? Nothing but the privilege to stay in the bomb shelter with your fear and resentments, imagining you're finally safe. Don't give in! Say, '*Fuck you*—I'm leaving the shelter and living my life!'"

"Jamie, I'm afraid . . . When I go to sleep, I still think of him and how he died—until then, I *did* have joy, there *wasn't* any bomb shelter. There weren't any bombs at all—"

"The pain of loss is the price of love. Without feeling that pain, you can't experience life's exuberance. The most important message to give yourself, Judy, is that you can *take* it; not only will you survive, you will *flourish.* You're not a teenager anymore; you're about to be married. It's time to forgive the universe, fate, or whatever for taking away your dad—and forgive *him* for dying on you. Forgive him for the secrets he kept about money that put your mom in such a terrible situation. Forgive *yourself* for the shame and embarrassment you felt as a kid over things you had zero control over. Life's asking you to make the transition into a deeper spiritual maturity."

I taught Judy the following Tool.

THE TOOL
The Blessing
(P.S.& J.R.)

Think of the person you can't forgive—the one you resent or even despise. Picture yourself kneeling on the ground in front of them, foreheads barely touching.

Say the words, "I bless you."

Say the words, "I forgive you."

With that, the Mother descends from above. She's a regal presence, sitting upon a golden throne. A cone of light emanates from below her as the she descends. The light encircles you and the person you kneel with.

The Mother is now just a few feet above you both. You and the person you cannot forgive are enclosed in her powerfully comforting, protective cone of light.

Inside this healing light, all resentment dissolves into a powerful feeling of goodwill.

You and your partner feel profoundly connected—your hearts overflow with the Mother's unconditional love.

Now, look outside the circle of light: A huge mass of people are watching the scene, transfixed by the miracle happening in front of them. In this moment, they have witnessed the transformational power of Love—they're learning by example.

You understand and see *that the mystical act of transmuting negativity into love has the power to affect the entire world.*

~

Stutz initially developed the above for dissolving resentments; my addition was the aspect of forgiveness. The Tool can be used to heal your enmity toward another person but also encourages self-forgiveness for past mistakes. The kneeling described is not an act of submission but of honoring the Mother, yourself, and the Other. It isn't an act of contrition either but one of acquiescence to various forces and energies, including those of Love. The Blessing Tool can also help with forgiveness of an event (like the plane crash that killed Judy's father). In that case, imagine kneeling down in front of the event itself and forgiving fate or whatever forces caused the terrible happening.

Remember, Madame X wants you to stay in resentment and "justified" anger. You'll hear her voice, throwing up obstacles: "Forgiveness is not only impossible, but *wrong*," or "Forgiveness means excusing evil! If you allow yourself to *forgive* Evil, you *become* Evil."

Redefining forgiveness is a typical MX makeover.

Let me repeat: *There is no way to understand or justify evil.* How do we forgive a monster? How do we even begin? A drunk driver who killed a loved one or someone who commits a violent act against your child . . . If you've experienced profound abuse or lost someone to the malevolent actions of another person, you don't have to forgive *the person themself.* As mentioned earlier, you can apply radical forgiveness to a cosmology where such darkness is "allowed" to occur.

The lights are low in the living room. You trip and fall; as a result, you lose the full use of your body. For months, you'd been meaning to tack down the carpet's edge but were too busy.

You too, then, are among the group of those who need to be forgiven.

Back to the frequent question: How do we forgive *ourselves*? Not just for wishing agony or even death on those who harmed us, but for tormenting ourselves over things we did or didn't do that have terrible results?

Radical forgiveness is the antidote for that poison, as you'll see in the following story.

~

My client Xavier was alone for the weekend. His wife was visiting her elderly parents.

Early Sunday morning, Xavier left his bed and went down the hall to use the bathroom. He tripped on a loose edge of the carpet, something he'd meant to fix. For weeks, he was careful where he stepped (his wife nimbly walked over it without a care), shaking his head each time with a smile at his talent for procrastination.

The fall knocked him out. When he came to, he was on his back, unable to move. Instantly, he knew that his neck was broken. A neighbor heard his screams and called 911.

I visited Xavier in the hospital. He was paralyzed from the neck down. He was on a respirator and was unable to speak. There was an alphabet board on his nightstand. I picked it up and we began to communicate. He blinked his eyes when I pointed to the right letter. He was a successful entertainment attorney—witty, acerbic, and super smart—and now we were playing a hellish version of charades. He was sixty years old and had just celebrated one year of sobriety.

Was this his reward?

He eventually regained his ability to speak and asked if we could have phone sessions. What could I tell him—"This too shall pass"? Because catastrophic injuries to the spine don't. Hopefully, there would be some improvement but there was no doubt that his life had changed forever. In those first few weeks, I simply encouraged him to stay alive, a day, an hour, a minute, a *moment* at a time.

Four years after his accident, some movement has returned. His hands can grip utensils when the food is on the wheelchair tray, but he's unable to walk. I no longer see him as a client. When we talk now, it's as friends. I called Xavier when I was writing this chapter and he enthusiastically wanted me to share some of our conversation.

Jamie: I wanted to talk to you about the really deep spiritual experience you've been forced to undergo in the last few years.

Xavier: Well, that's true. I can't imagine going through what I did *without* having a spiritual experience. I can't contemplate how one could do that. I'd have to go back and look at the calendar, but—I don't know—I think it was a year or so into being sober that I came out of unconsciousness into a new reality. Then, in the hospital, I came out of *another* kind of unconsciousness into *another* new reality. I'll never forget when my sponsor came to the hospital that first time. He sat with me and read the serenity prayer out loud. "God grant me the serenity to accept the things I cannot change." And I'm truly blessed that my wife has been a spiritual seeker all her life and is deeply imbued with serious knowledge. And *you* came—and reminded me of the Tools. What stayed with me most was the idea of the String of Pearls. That stays with me to this day. I mean, String of Pearls is a way of life. So I came home and began physical therapy and the process of whatever—getting real with my new body. And a couple of months later, my wife arranged for me to take some classes in meditation. I was given a mantra. And again, that just became part of a giant piece of . . . I'll call it "recovery," and it stays with me. It stays. I found myself spending my waking hours, and for all I knew, my sleeping hours too, engaged in let's call it spiritual work. More engaged than I had ever been in my entire life. I'm meditating all the time and have become much more involved in my religious community; my rabbi's come to see me. I'm sober and rereading the Tools. After I fell, the Stutz documentary came out. It really hit home when he taught that Reversal of Desire tool—where you say to the pain, "Bring it on!" I've thought of that so often! It's not just that particular one that helps, but really *all* the Tools—and the meditation—even the weird rhythm of physical therapy, the struggle of physical therapy. Through it all, I kept saying to myself, "Bring it on!" I can't tell you how many times I've used that phrase. When Part X got really strong in me, sometimes I'd use Cosmic Rage. I had this spectacular first year of physical therapy. I mean, *unbelievable* progress. But the nature of spinal cord injuries are devilish—they don't 'behave.' You are *not* proceeding along a straight line. You're on a rollercoaster. Your body and mood take huge dips and you're thinking, "I'm on track to be walking with a cane soon!"—but no, you're *not.* You're back in your wheelchair. So, it was essential for me to rely on and *deepen* those spiritual practices. They were all I had—maybe it's all any of us have. And that's going to be true forever. I don't know. I don't. All things considered, there's no question that every one of these practices are really helping. I mean, I shouldn't be this happy! I *shouldn't* be, Jamie, but I am."

Xavier is a living example of radical acceptance and forgiveness. The act of radical forgiveness requires a complete surrender to the *I-can't-know-ness* of life. If your heart feels broken, it means you're doing it right.

Your heart *has* broken—*open.*

~

We all begin as a bundle of bones lost somewhere in a desert,
a dismantled skeleton that lies under the sand.
It is our work to put the bones together.
—Clarissa Pinkola Estés

Health is not about having normal insulin levels or clear margins.
True healing is cycling between death and rebirth. You have to
keep letting yourself be killed and then returning to light.
—Phil Stutz

The Sick Shadow

In chapters 4 and 5, I discussed the Inferior and Evil Shadows, but there is one more—the most esoteric of the shadows—the Sick Shadow.

The Sick Shadow descends from the spiritual realm of pure light and when we are born, sacrifices itself by entering our bodies. The shadow is "sick" because it has been relegated to a world without light: earthly existence, the domain of mortality. It has done so for a profound reason, that of becoming a conduit to the eternal part of ourselves.

Stutz has Parkinson's and frequently experiences a symptom called "freezing of gait." When it happens, he has the uncanny feeling that his feet, quite literally, are stuck to the floor. In order take a step forward, he'll sometimes drop to his knees and crawl. Reflecting on those moments, he says, "Everyone who is really sick can reach a level of despondency where they don't see a way out. But there is a way out—through *inner death*."

The Sick Shadow serves us in that way. It allows us to cycle through death and rebirth so that, however briefly, we're allowed access to the soulful, immortal part of ourselves. Such is the poignant, ineffable sacrifice of the Sick Shadow. It has no home. Over and over, it drops down from the eternal into the mortal world of birth, illness, and death.

A few months after my father's passing, a dark pink, ragged spot about the size of a fingernail appeared on the left side of my chest (as a redhead, I'm always on high alert). The biopsy showed that it was melanoma. We caught it early enough that it was still in situ, or surface-depth. The only consequence was a five-inch scar. Given the all clear, I went back to life as usual.

Then I started forgetting things.

It's fairly typical of me to misplace my phone around the house or have that where-the eff-are-my-effing keys moment. What *wasn't* typical was standing up friends for lunch or missing a weekly session with a client whom I'd been seeing for years. I got spooked. I went straight to "Ask not for whom the dementia tolls. . . ." Then, on a day that I was beating myself up for flaking on a speaking engagement, an extraordinary image came to me. It was a character from the Japanese theatrical form called Noh. In my mind, I saw a woman in a white robe with long black hair. She wore a mask with pinpoint eyes and straight brows, giving the expression of fear. Her painted mouth was shaped in a red O—a distorted, silent, frozen howl—she was an image of pure grief. The vision was so powerful that I sank to the floor of my living room and sobbed. The anguished woman in white seemed to express everything that was bottled up inside me. I stayed with her, crying on my knees for a long while.

Crouching in the depths, I wept on the Underworld floor and allowed myself to experience seemingly bottomless, excruciating grief. When I finally rose, exhausted but whole, an almost supernatural sense of calm overtook me. I felt present and connected to the world. After the "visitation," my bout of forgetting ended. I still had great sadness but the Lady in White—the Sick Shadow—helped me evolve into a new self, one whose identity assimilated the loss of my Dad. This is how the Sick Shadow gives true healing. It connects us with the inextricably linked poles of mortal death and aliveness, reminding that there is no joy without sorrow, no health without sickness, no pleasure without pain, no darkness without light.

As a melanin-deficient redhead, I like to bone up on all things having to do with skin. During one of my forays, I learned that researchers found a link between the suppression of emotions and the occurrence of melanoma (and other cancers). Seven years after Dad died, my mother joined him.

A few months later, I was diagnosed with a second melanoma, again in situ.

Like the other Shadow figures, it's essential to connect with our Sick Shadow. Unexpressed grief, like suppressed anger and resentment, has a cost. If we don't make space for it, we won't have the resources to pay the energetic bill.

How to Connect with the Sick Shadow

The Sick Shadow is unlike the other shadow figures. We can bond to other shadows with words, but the Sick Shadow is unique because words are foreign to it. The Sick Shadow *only connects energetically*, through feelings.

There isn't a fixed way to work with this Shadow. The process is different for everyone. One of the techniques I offer to clients is creating a space of Sacred Ritual.

~

EXERCISE
The Sacred Space
(J.R.)

Find a time and space where you can be alone. Darken the room. Light a candle, burn incense. If it moves you, play some soothing or soul-stirring music—or remain in silence.

Adopt a position of surrender. For me, it's kneeling with my hands in front of my chest in Anjali mudra (palms together in prayer), with my forehead touching the ground. It's almost like being in the yogic Child's Pose. Some may feel it more natural to lay down and face upward, with a blanket or pillow, in the pose called Savasana. Others will gravitate toward movement, perhaps even dance. Gabriella Roth's Five Rhythms is a wonderful practice to accompany that.

Some of my clients simply write in their journal, letting thoughts and words flow. In that regard, try to write without stopping for at least a few minutes. An alternate approach is to ask a question with your dominant hand, then answer it with your non-dominant one.

If an image doesn't come, as it did for me with the Lady in White, no worries at all. Simply connect with the part of you that feels broken. Which of course means broken open.

Don't try to understand the Sick shadow intellectually. That's impossible. Just *feel* her. If you give her time—if you're willing to break open—she will find you, and always be there for you.

Always.

The Sick Shadow will help you to see that the experiences of illness, loss, and grief serve a spiritual purpose. Those events are teachers that give your life a deeper meaning and value.

Loss

In the years since Mom and Dad passed, I've gone through more loss—close friends and members of my extended family. Some of them were much younger than me. And just yesterday, as of this writing, my beloved cat of sixteen years died in my arms. My dear, dear Fenway.

The theme of my seventh decade of life has become all about letting go.

When my mother died, she left an apartment full of things—porcelain figurines, bags of costume jewelry from Chico's, clothes she bought at the "Last Call!" department of Macy's. Some still had tags. (When I complimented her on a new shirt or pair of pants, instead of saying thank you, she'd shout, "Only $6.99 with my coupon!") We donated most of Reta's things to her favorite charity shops, but I kept a few pieces of jewelry Dad gave her over the years. And some of her favorite blouses. Photos of our huge family were all over the walls; ancestors long-dead, and cousins and siblings, a lot of whom left the earth during the twenty-five years that my folks lived there—the place, that for eight years anyway, was "just down the hall." The closets were stacked with memory boxes. There were gorgeous pictures of Reta and Stewart Rose, some of them taken backstage, impromptu, while others were more formal or posed. They were so young and glamorous in their show biz days! Like people do, I sent them off to be digitized. I still have boxes of photographs in storage because I ran out of digitizing steam.

When I die, where will those memories go? To my brother? My nephews? Will they save them to look at once or twice before slowly filling their own closets with forgotten images? Will those old school prints end up being sold for a dollar in a thrift shop because they're "kitsch?" And what about the journals I'd been keeping since I was little? My very first one, with the tiny gold lock and the satin cover embossed with flowers . . . all my stories.

All my identities, my different professions.

All my moods.

My loves, my tears, my changing body . . .

All the people I loved—and those who loved me, many of them now gone or on their way.

The older I get, the more I am in touch with the soul part of myself that will never die. Like my friend Xavier, my spiritual connection has become profoundly essential. *That* is the value of connecting to the pure spirit of the Sick Shadow. Triggered by illness and grief, she descends to sacrifice herself so that, again and again, we may be reborn. One day, this body will be gone—like the Sick shadow, I will return to that perfect, etheric place from which we all came.

The space where there is no loss, no separateness, no death. A space of pure love.

THE TOOL
Islands
(B.M.)[8]

Picture yourself and your Shadow sitting together on a small island floating on a calm sea. A few yards in front of you is another island; on it, is the person you're attached to. Your islands are connected by a thin strip of land.

Look at the person you're attached to with as much longing and desire as you can. You want them with every fiber of your being. You feel like you will die if you can't have them.

The islands begin to drift away from each other. As they do, the strip of land connecting you begins to stretch. Soon, the stretching strip of land becomes so thin that it breaks.

The island on which your beloved sits continues to drift away, becoming smaller and smaller until it finally disappears over the horizon. You feel an aching sense of loss.

Now, turn toward your Shadow—and give it all those feelings of desire and longing you felt for the person on the other island.

You and your Shadow now feel deeply connected and whole.

[8] Barry Michels wrote this Tool with the Inferior Shadow in mind, but you may also use the Sick Shadow.

That is the paradox of life—everything is gained from letting go.

Chapter Ten

HIPA and the Divine Feminine

I learned to make my mind large, as the universe is large,
so that there is room for paradoxes.
—Maxine Hong Kingston, *The Woman Warrior*

I'm the piece of shit the world revolves around.
—Anonymous

Phil Stutz has a guiding philosophy called HIPA—Humility, Ignorance, Poverty, and Anonymity. He's called the acronym an "operating system for life."

Let's talk about humility.

An embarrassing amount of my downtime is spent watching cat videos on Instagram. Also, since I have two of them (three when I began writing this book), I will literally be draped in cats while watching videos of cats. Hey, there are *worse* addictions, many of which I've partaken in, but I'll never be feline sober. Anyway, the Insta algorithm knows me very well. This morning, it provided a perfect metaphor: a video of a tiny kitten desperately clawing at its cage to get out. If it had only turned to its right, it would have found that the door to the cage was wide open. But the kitty thought that if it could only tear down the bars in front of her, she'd be free. Many of us are just like that—we can only see "one way out," until a simple change of perspective shows us the way.

In my actress days, I thought stardom would fill the gaping hole inside me. Other times, my "fix" was a romantic relationship or homeownership or having (or not having) a child. It's important to have goals and desires, but there's a danger in becoming too attached. When we fixate on the notion that there's only *one* path, *one* way—that must be followed at all costs—then we risk being trapped in a cage (that isn't really a cage at all).

Humility is what helps free us from the illusion that we're trapped. At its core, humility keeps the ego in check. I'm not a god, I'm just a human. It's impossible to have all the answers, for myself or for you. Since I can't know in advance the outcome of an event, I can't know the action that's best for me. The only path is to push forward and make the best decision with the information at hand. It's easy to get stuck. So many times we become paralyzed, fearful of taking the wrong fork in the road (or mistaking that fork for a spoon). Since we can't try out multiple choices in alternate realities, we can never know if the "road not taken" was in fact better than the one you set out on. Only God, the Universe, and Time will tell how things work out. In fact, sometimes the "wrong" path leads to the right one.

But there's a big difference between humility and humiliation.

Telling yourself "I'm the lowest of the low" is just as prideful as announcing "I'm the greatest." There's a saying in twelve-step groups: "I'm the piece of shit the world revolves around." When I look back at the cringe mistakes I've made, it's essential to give myself grace, and make amends. When I did unkind or stupid stuff, I was doing the best I could at the level of spiritual development that I had at the time. Likewise, everyone else is doing their best. When a person is short with me or humblebrags or lets me down in whatever way, my first reaction is often judge-y and self-righteous. But if I take a moment to ask if I've ever done just as they have (or my own customized version), the answer's usually yes. That's often why it stings.

True power is anchored in humility, a word too often misused. The humility I speak of doesn't apply to the self-deprecating "modesty" most women are socialized into having—but one that is *right-sized* and defined by our surrender to the conviction, "I am exactly who I am. I have the wisdom, strength and resolution required to leave the cage through the open door." If I pretend I'm *less-than*, that's pride in reverse—simply the other side of the same prideful coin.

The Buddhist nun, Pema Chödrön sums this idea up beautifully in the following excerpt from her book *Start Where You Are: A Guide to Compassionate Living*:

> I was invited to teach in a situation with the Sawang, Trungpa Rinpoche's eldest son, in which it wasn't exactly clear what my status was. Sometimes I was treated as a big deal who should come in through a

> special door and sit in a special seat. Then I'd think, "Okay, I'm a big deal." I'd start running with that idea and come up with big-deal notions about how things should be, and then I'd get the messages back, "Oh, no, no, no. You should just sit on the floor and mix with everybody and be one of the crowd." Okay. So now the message was that I should just be ordinary, not set myself up or be the teacher. But as soon as I was getting comfortable with being humble, I would be asked to do some special something or other that only big deals did. This was a painful experience because I was always being insulted and humiliated by my own expectations. As soon as I was sure how it should be, so I could feel secure, I would get a message that it should be the other way. Finally I said to the Sawang, "This is really hurting. I just don't know who I'm supposed to be," and he said, *"Well, you have to learn to be big and small at the same time."*[9]

Humility can be experienced as a state that is sometimes called Flow—a place of indifference where one is able to be completely present in the current moment. Madame X wants us to believe in a world where everything is black or white, good or bad, true or false.

That world is an illusion.

---

[9] From *Start Where You Are: A Guide to Compassionate Living* by Pema Chödrön. Copyright ©1994 by Pema Chödrön. Reprinted by arrangement with The Permissions Company LLC on behalf of Shambhala Publications Inc., Boulder, Colorado, www.shambhala.com.

Flow is the space of creativity—a nonbinary realm that reflects essential reality—a world where, as Chödrön illustrated in her story, you are "big and small at the same time."

THE TOOL
Category Three
(P.S.)

Close your eyes and conjure a strong feeling of LOVE.

Let it go.

Now conjure a strong feeling of RAGE.

Let it go.

Cycle through again.

Feel intense LOVE.

Let that go.

Now, intense RAGE.

Let it go.

Cycle through both emotions once more.

Feel intense LOVE.

Let it go.

Now, RAGE.

Let that go.

Now, trigger BOTH FEELINGS, TOGETHER.

Let that go.

Again—

BOTH FEELINGS, TOGETHER.

You are now in Category Three.

At first, this Tool may feel strange and uncomfortable. Even impossible. Which, in a way, it is. At the end of the Tool, you aren't feeling love or hate—you've entered a unique ontological mode called Category Three. What you're feeling is called *Flow*, where there is no past or future, only the present.

To be in Flow is to be in a state of humility. In Flow, you have access to a deep wisdom, one that isn't based on facts, intellect, or emotion, but a wisdom infused by the creative—a *feeling wisdom* that's fluid and promotes inspired thought and action. Such wisdom is *archetypally feminine* in nature. In Flow, you're big and small; not the best and not the worst. You've escaped the human realm of hierarchies.

You're not only, as Stutz says, "the one who puts the next pearl on the string"—you're the pearl itself.

~

In the beginner's mind there are many possibilities,
but in the expert's there are few.
—Shunryu Suzuki, *Zen Mind, Beginners Mind*

Ignorance is bliss.
—Thomas Gray

Ignorance

Plato famously wrote that "wonder is the beginning of all philosophy." Wonder leads us from the physical world into that of the spiritual—what Stutz calls Universe Two. Plato was a mystic;

for him, true reality existed behind the veil of the material world (Stutz's Universe One). He believed that the most important knowledge was a priori, rising within from remembered truths the soul knew before birth. In contrast, his student Aristotle laid the foundation for the scientific method. For Aristotle, ignorance was a problem to a be solved by proper investigation that would reveal the right answer. Stutz calls being "right" the booby prize. (No shade on Aristotle!)

Spiritual ignorance means living in a state of open-minded innocence. The Zen Buddhists call it *shoshin* or "beginner's mind." *Shoshin* is a way of being that doesn't require an answer. It is a state of exquisite curiosity, the blissful I-don't-knowness discussed earlier in this book.

Near the turn of the nineteenth century, the world was entranced by a Native American amed Ishi who'd spent his life isolated in the California wilderness. In 1911, this last known member of the Yahi Yana tribe emerged from isolation and was set upon by hordes of anthropologists. When he saw his first steam locomotive, snaking along, bellowing smoke and fire, he believed the train was a demon. Ishi got onboard, anyway.

When asked why, he said, "My life has taught me to be more curious than afraid."

~

Here are some meditations that can help you enter a state of wonder.

THE TOOL
Dissolving Thought
(P.S.)

Look around your environment. You're surrounded by objects—now, imagine you suddenly have no idea of their meaning. For example, you're in your living room. There may be a shelf of books. A potted plant. A chair. But you have no idea what these objects represent. They are merely forms, without identity or purpose. Notice their color, their contours. But don't identify them as shelf, books, plant, or chair.

Madame X will rebel against this process. She'll say, "No! That is a chair! That is a plant! This is stupid!" Do it anyway.

Now, close your eyes, remembering the forms you've seen. Then, like the famous clocks in Salvador Dalí's paintings, see them begin to melt.

The objects in the room liquefy and melt together like a box of crayons left in the sun.

Now, you *are melting too—and join this mass of melting and melted objects.*

As a part of this formless, nameless mass, you feel whole. A sense of profound connectedness overtakes you. This is a space of no thinking. There are no opinions here. There is only presence. Only acceptance.

THE TOOL
Awe
(P.S. & J.R.)

Close your eyes and imagine you're in the high mountains on a clear night. You peer up at the black sky, dotted by a limitless canopy of stars.

As you stare into the sky, you feel a sense of benevolence—as if this vast, silent, unspeakably beautiful universe is in love with you.

Now, imagine a well of emotion rising in you—frustration, anger, sadness—at the feeling of being separate from the immensity and grandeur of the universe above.

Send all of that emotion up into the star-filled sky.

As you do, the stars flash. Then you feel the light of the celestial bodies rain down and enter your heart. As it does, you begin to feel peace. The heavy, blocking emotions are gone. There is only stillness and majesty now.

As you gaze into that vast sky, you are filled with humility and grace.

You understand that you are and have always been a small part of this glorious universe.

Poverty

If you build a chair in the material world, it's there the next morning. If you build a chair in the spiritual world, it's not. You have to build it again.

That's what Stutz means by poverty—*spiritual* poverty. The maintenance and pursuit of a sound spiritual condition is made by ceaseless effort. A common error is to feel that one has "graduated" (*I've worked all the Tools, I did a silent meditation retreat, I mastered the Scorpion Pose*) and is now free to abandon spiritual pursuits. But just as we don't expect to remain fit by going to the gym a few times a year, it's the same with our spiritual condition. The discipline required for its evolution is a lifelong commitment. Things do get easier—once you get a taste of what it feels like to be in the world with open-mindedness, gratitude, and serenity, that's where you want to live.

The Tools that expand the practice of spiritual poverty are *any* of the meditations and exercises I've discussed. The sheer intent and *willingness* to work a Tool is in itself an act of spiritual discipline.

Keep stringing those pearls . . .

Anonymity

You don't get extra points for being on a spiritual path. No gold stars or trophies are awarded for facing conflict with equanimity and emotional maturity. No one can know how hard you're working to keep the she-wolf Madame X at bay. The spiritual work you do will become a way of life—it is a commitment you make to yourself, to yourself only. You don't need to be noticed or appreciated for your efforts. It simply becomes how you choose to move through the world, with elegance, grace, and purpose. Living a spiritually connected life aligns you with the energy of the Universe. The paradox is that the more contained your ego becomes, the greater your potential.

Like the unruly kitten, let your ego bang at the door of the cage while you make your great escape.

~

> For old people, beauty doesn't come free with the hormones the way it does for the young. It has to do with bones. It has to do with who the person is . . . it has to do with what shines through those gnarly faces and bodies.
>
> —Ursula K. Le Guin

A Visible Woman

Many women talk about becoming invisible when they're older. I saw this happen with my mother when I took her to doctor's offices. It was as if they didn't care or just dismissed her—why waste their time when she was so close to the grave? Mom died from bladder cancer; despite multiple visits to urologists, it went undiagnosed for a year. There's a scarcity of female urologists, so the ones I tried were booked out months in advance. I couldn't get an appointment. The offices of the male doctors we ended up in were papered with diagrams of penises and testicles—there wasn't a cervix, uterus, or female urinary tract to be found. The enlarged prostate was the flag that waved. When Reta died, I got in touch with each of those men to call them out on their erasure of women; to my surprise, with compassion, they promised to correct the egregious oversight.

Some of the invisibility that aging confers is welcome (no more catcalls and leering on the street) and even comes as a relief. Like all women, I spent decades routinely having my face and body appraised by those I didn't know; being an actress, those appraisals felt like they were multiplied a thousandfold. Casting directors, producers, and network executives looked me over to assess whether I was pretty enough, thin enough, young enough—all code for the industry's sliding "fuckable" scale when it came to being cast in a lead role. In the '80s, I did a screen test for an Aaron Spelling show where all the actresses were told *in writing* to wear tights and leotards (think Jane Fonda in her aerobics years) but *not* leg warmers because "they can hide a multitude of sins." Since entering my sixties, my body's definitely changed. I do strength-training exercises several times a week, but the skin on my upper arms seems to rebel against looking *toned*.

Everything's rebelling.

Madame X wants me to hate the inevitable, bullying me to cover my body and hide its perceived flaws from the world. *Ain't gonna happen.* I've become respectful, loving, and gentle to my "old lady" shadow self—honoring the chameleon form that's loyally served me since birth. My body has always taken care of me and now it's important I take care of *her*, as a child would her mother. Now, looking at my age spots during a manicure, I see my mother's hands. Touching my upper arm, I'm reminded of my Grandma Sally; when I was little, I loved the feel of her soft skin.

Invisibility isn't just a phenomenon faced by older women. If your identity and self-worth is dependent on how you're perceived by the world, you can feel invisible at any age. Young women who try to make themselves exemplify the aesthetic ideals of whatever current beauty trends can feel just as invisible as a white-haired octogenarian. Lillian Hellman had that great quote, "I cannot and will not cut my conscience to fit this year's fashions"—well, I'm not willing to do that either when it comes to the precious vessel that has walked me through this life.

To be a visible woman, our sense of value must come from within.

~

> What is the greatest lesson a woman should learn?
> That since day one, she's already
> had everything she needs within herself.
> It's the world that convinced her she did not.
> —Rupi Kaur

> If you try to erase who I am, I will write myself back in.
> —Janelle Monáe

Another Shadow

I've already introduced you to the three shadows in Stutz's teachings: Inferior, Evil, and Sick. In my ongoing work with myself and clients, I've discovered more.

Let's meet the Aspirational Shadow.

EXERCISE
The Aspirational Shadow
(J.R.)

Take out your journal and write down the names of three to five women you admire, living or dead, real or fictional.

To stir your imagination, here are a handful of names my clients came up with—Mae West, Shirley Chisholm, Gloria Steinem, Louise Bourgeois, "Annie Savoy" (from the movie *Bull Durham*), Beyoncé, and Malala Yousafzai.

Here's one of my own lists:

Michelle Yeoh
Ursula K. Le Guin
Maya Angelou
Furiosa (from the Mad Max film series)
Janelle Monáe

Write down three qualities you admire most about each woman on your list. It's important to note that the person, whether fictional or real, may not actually possess the characteristics you attribute to them. That doesn't matter at all for this exercise. We are only interested in how you *perceive* them. Don't think about it too much! Just write down the most prominent traits that come to mind.

Using my list, here are my impressions:

Michelle Yeoh: Fit and agile. Authentically gorgeous. Exudes feminine strength.

Ursula K. Le Guin: Brilliant writer. Embodies my ideal of mature womanhood. Great sense of humor.

Maya Angelou: Fully inhabits and celebrates her sensuality. Unapologetically powerful. Moves and speaks with a slow feline grace.

Furiosa: Uses intellectual resourcefulness rather than brute strength to achieve her goals. (Brute strength when necessary!) Fierce protector of the vulnerable. And so cool looking.

Janelle Monáe: Explosively talented and charismatic. Drop-dead personal style. Does not hide who she is.

Now, pick out one of the names from your list.

Close your eyes.

Imagine a version of yourself that has the qualities you wrote down. Make her as specific as you can. What does she look like? How is she dressed? How is her hair styled? Is she standing or sitting? Is she lying down?

Work with this Shadow the way you would with any of your Shadows—enter into a relationship with her. Is there anything she wants you to know?

There's a reason you picked the women you did. The characteristics that you admire in the people you've chosen are unrealized, disowned qualities that you yourself *already possess*—or wish to.

The next Tool gives you a taste of what it would feel like to move through the world as the woman you aspire to be.

THE TOOL
Aspirational Inhabitation
(J.R.)

Close your eyes.

Pretend it's Halloween or that you're on your way to a masquerade party. Imagine you've put on a full-body costume of the person you admire.

You're still you*—the outfit is like a stained glass window—and your soul is the light shining through.*

Now, think of a past event or interaction where you wish you'd behaved differently. As if reshooting a scene in a movie, redo this "happening" by seeing yourself behave with the aspirational qualities *of the woman you admire.*[10]

You now have a template.

And you can put on the "costume" anytime you like.

[10] The "redoing" is an adaptation of Phil Stutz's "Principle of Correction" described on page 121.

~

It is imperative that women reclaim our precious energy
so we can bring forward the feminine principle,
the Divine Feminine, with the full force required
to rebalance society's ills.
—Elise Loehnen, *On Our Best Behavior: The Price Women Pay to Be Good*

Divine(ly) Feminine Power

For thousands of years, divinity has been cast in the shape of a man: usually a bearded patriarch in the clouds. But long before Yahweh thundered from Sinai or Zeus hurled lightning from Olympus, the divine was imagined—worshipped—as female. Archaeological findings from 30,000 BCE reveal voluptuous goddess figures carved in stone and bone, representing fertility, regeneration, and the mysterious alchemy of this astonishing, magical life. The Great Mother was not subordinate to any male god—she was the Source.

The origin.

The totality . . .

Theologically (and biologically), this makes sense. Life literally begins in the female body; we gestate inside a woman. Our earliest experience of the divine is not the judgmental father in the sky but the enveloping, nourishing darkness of the womb. The Hebrew word for the breath of life, *ruach*, is grammatically feminine. It was *she* who inspired the words "Let there be light" and stirred the Void into becoming; the spirit of God, from the very beginning, was Her.

Modern science also reveals an unexpected poetry. In embryonic development, the human body begins with the potential to become female. In the absence of specific genetic instructions (the SRY gene on the Y chromosome), the body proceeds along the female developmental path. In other words, femaleness is the biological default. If we're to read this not just as biology but as metaphor, it becomes revelatory: the Divine Feminine becomes the origin story and *original force*. Cyclical, generative, and enduring, she is the dark matter of divinity, the pulse beneath the patriarchal mask.

She is the matrix.

She is the mystery.

She is the unspoken Name.

~

I found god in myself & i loved her/i loved her fiercely.
—Ntozake Shange, *for colored girls who have considered suicide/when the rainbow is enuf*

The Goddess is the whole world, the source of all life, and the ultimate mystery of transformation.
—Marija Gimbutas

The Empress

To prepare for a women's workshop I was giving, I did some deep reading about the myth of Persephone, who was abducted by Hades, god of the underworld. Her mother, Demeter—goddess of harvest, grain, and fertility—was so aggrieved that she refused to allow crops to grow, creating famine on earth. But Zeus and the other Olympians required human prayers and sacrifices, so he ordered Hades to return Persephone to her mother. Hades agreed, but before giving her back, he tricked Persephone into eating some pomegranate seeds. According to ancient law, ingesting food from the underworld bound one to it; hence, Persephone was forced to return to Hades six months out of every year.

I like to keep a few oracle decks around my workspace for inspiration. Just before teaching the workshop, I accidentally knocked over a stack of Rider-Waite tarot cards. One of them fell face up, revealing a golden-haired woman on a majestic throne: The Empress. She wore a twelve-pointed crown, each point topped by a jewel signifying the twelve months and twelve astrological signs. In this deck, the gown of the Empress is festooned by what I had always thought were red flowers. On closer look, I saw that they were in fact . . . pomegranates.

The Divine Feminine had paid me a visit.

She inspired me to write the following Tool. I call it The Empress, but when you practice it, work with whatever goddess image resonates: Aphrodite, Oshun, Lakshmi. And don't be afraid of the "darker" goddesses like Durga or Baba Yaga. Maybe Persephone wasn't tricked at all when she ate those pomegranate seeds. It's possible she swallowed the fruit of the underworld on purpose. Perhaps she longed to dive into the shadowy, Stygian depths.[11]

[11] If you're looking for inspiration and guidance, I enthusiastically recommend two powerful resources: *The Goddess Oracle* by Amy Sophia Marashinsky and *The Divine Feminine Oracle* by Meggan Watterson. Both offer rich, insightful introductions to a wide range of feminine deities.

THE TOOL
The Empress
(J.R.)

Close your eyes and think of your favorite goddess or symbol of the divine feminine force. See her glowing with essential power and inner beauty. A radiant field of energy surrounds her that expands until it embraces you.

Enveloped in that embrace, you and the goddess—an icon of female power and magnificence—merge. You become one.

Open your eyes but keep the feeling of power and connection you experienced when your eyes were closed.

Move through the world embodied by this feeling. Wherever you go, you radiate the Divine Feminine force.

~

From start to finish, keep a constant gaze on the divine.
Live in devotion to this ever elusive mystery.
—Julie Piatt/SriMati

Have you ever heard the terms "left brain" and "right brain"? The phrases come from a theory popularized by the neuropsychologist Roger Sperry, whose research showed that the brain's left hemisphere processes language, logic, and analytical thinking, while the right hemisphere governs spatial abilities, facial recognition, and creativity. His studies led to the oversimplified idea that people were either left-brained (logical, analytical) or right-brained (creative, intuitive).

Sounds a bit like Masculine vs Feminine archetypes, right?

This theory of strict separation of brain functions has since been refuted. Contemporary neuroscience emphasizes that in nearly all cognitive functions, *both hemispheres work together*. Rather than being split into two discrete "types," science now views those hemispheres as interconnected and collaborative. Although in the preceding pages I've leaned into the feminine or so-called right-brained aspects of Source, I believe divinity to be limitless, ineffable, and genderless. As discussed throughout *Facing Madame X*, divinity encompasses the complete interconnectedness of female and male energetics—the yin and yang, the dance of sun and moon.

Abraham Maslow presented a basic hierarchy of needs—physiological (food, water, sleep); safety (security, shelter); love and belonging (relationships, connection); esteem (respect, confidence); and self-actualization (personal growth, fulfillment). Yet, once those needs are met, a problem often remains: the lack of connection with the Divine. Meeting life's challenges (loss of a job, rejection by a beloved, a protracted illness) with the determination to come away with a *teaching* is how we begin to develop courage and willpower. By doing so, we take a step on the path toward trusting ourselves. We know we may get knocked down but will rise up a little faster each time, and not just on the earthly plane; our resurrections bring us ever closer to the plane of the celestial.

In this way, one's entire life becomes an initiatory experience into the Divine.

Madame X isn't a fan of interconnectedness. She wants me to tell you that only the *Feminine* energetic is the true source of power; she wants me to say that *real* power can only be found through the *Masculine*; she wants me to strongly suggest that only through a *genderless* looking-glass can we understand who and what we really are.

Madame X hates wonder and I-don't-knowness; she exhorts me to offer tidy *conclusions*. She promotes *certainty, knowing-ness*. She's nurtured by it and propagandizes for it.

But what do conclusions and certainty give us?

Separation . . .

~

The Tools and stories I've presented in *Facing Madame X* can be used as both a reminder and guide, invoking a power that is strong enough to hold dichotomies and paradoxes, darkness and light.

Only by unifying our divinely disparate parts, may we transcend; only through the cosmic can we know, or begin to know, what it means to be human. My work with Phil Stutz opened the door to such understanding. Encounters with Madame X did the same, pushing me to hone myself like the blade of a knife being sharpened by a whetstone. I needed to cultivate an *awareness*—not just of MX's presence but of her purpose. In Stutz's metaphor, I had to go down that road without veering into a ditch or oncoming traffic; learn when to speed up or slow down, and when to go *around* the obstacles that sprang up.

As our days are divided by sleep and wakefulness—by ordinary activity and night-dreaming, by common and uncommon yearnings—women, like Persephone unbound, must choose to live, not in combat, but alongside their Shadows and the brightness that creates them.

I wish that for you with all my heart.

Acknowledgments

To my parents, who, through it all, always made us feel loved and valued. And especially to the great Reta Rose, for not only giving me permission but encouraging me to tell our unfiltered story.

To my brother Stephen—for giving me a second chance at being your loving older sister.

To Meli, for literally sharing the load during and after our mother's death.

To my nephews Justin, Brendan, and Ethan—you are spectacular in every way.

To my stepdaughter Morgan, stepson PJ, and step-grandchildren Marlowe and Leon—thank you for letting me be your "GramJam."

With deep love to my treasured cousin-sister Susan West, who, by her example with her husband, my dear Ray, showed me what real partnership looks like—and made me believe I was worth it.

My sweet Fenway, my fur-son, thank you for fifteen years of the sweetest love and devotion. You will always be alive in my heart.

Tony Lyons, I'm profoundly grateful for your fearless support of the written word and your belief in this book. I love you. You're family.

Stephan Zguta, you're a force of nature. Your brilliance and unwavering diligence leave me in awe.

To Jim Krusoe, who taught me how to write, and Samantha Dunn, who told me I could do it—again.

To Lynn Johnston for early support, and to Sara Carder for your invaluable hand in shaping the proposal for this book.

To Sue Campbell for the "variation" that sparked its inspiration, and to Anne Hawley for the "Writer's Sprint."

To my soul-brother Michael Lally—for forty years of friendship, wisdom, and fierce loyalty.

To Sue, Jeanne, and Spencer for our Wednesday "gatherings," and to the women of *Saturdays at 10 a.m.*—your honesty, humor, and kindness are a constant source of strength and joy.

To Allison Anders—my queen, my twenty-minutes-a-day sister (we did it!)—and to the real-life goddess Julie Piatt, another sister on the Plane of Will. Gold stars for us all!

To the brilliant-beyond-her-years Sarai Jimenez, for friendship and steadfast support, and to Hilary Wheeler, for wisdom, laughter, and newsletter rescue (time for you to write your book!).

To all of my clients—for initiating me into my own divine(ly) feminine power.

Barry Michels, you are tender, compassionate, and possess a poet's soul. I, and everyone who has had the honor of your attention and care, are indeed blessed.

Phil Stutz, my teacher, brother, father, friend. Words can't touch the depth of my gratitude and love for you. You quite literally saved my life and helped me create a new one—one that fulfills me in ways I never thought possible. You made me a better human. Having said that, I'll probably never be able to shut the f**k up.

And lastly—and always—to my beloved husband, Bruce: editor, coach, teacher, joke sweetener, and in-house (sometimes in-bed) writing staff. Senior love is the best love—'til death do us part.

I don't want to get to the end of my life and find that I have just lived the length of it. I want to have lived the width of it as well.

—Diane Ackerman